THE MANAGEMENT OF LOSS

Loss is experienced in many forms—from the death of a loved one, illness, and job loss, to the emotional turmoil surrounding retirement, divorce, separation, or even the quiet ache of boredom and loneliness. World-renowned leadership scholar, psychoanalyst, social psychologist, and executive coach Manfred Kets de Vries explores how we can navigate loss in both life and work.

A pioneer in the field of clinical and psychodynamic-systemic executive coaching, Manfred examines a wide spectrum of losses—some obvious, others more subtle—shedding light on how we respond to them. Some people fight against loss, denying its reality at all costs. Others may become consumed by grief. For some, work becomes a coping mechanism, a way to manage the existential anxiety that stems from life's impermanence. In such cases, "manic" work habits can become a distraction—an escape from confronting painful truths. Written in an accessible and conversational style—as if speaking with a group of friends—this book offers deeply human insights brought to life through personal anecdotes, case studies, and illustrative vignettes. Manfred encourages readers to face their inner struggles without falling back on primitive defense mechanisms like splitting, projection, or denial. He guides us in reflecting on the consequences of our choices—past and future—so we may recognize our limitations, embrace our potential, and find meaning amid loss.

An essential read for anyone grappling with loss, this book is especially valuable for executives, executive coaches, consultants, self-help enthusiasts, and well-being practitioners.

Manfred F. R. Kets de Vries is the Distinguished Clinical Professor of Leadership Development and Organizational Change at INSEAD, as well as the founder of INSEAD's Global Leadership Centre. Recognized globally as one of the foremost thinkers in management, he has been featured by leading publications such as *The Financial Times*, *Wirtschaftswoche*, *Le Capital*, *El País*, and *The Economist*. He is the author of more than 60 books and hundreds of articles, and has received multiple prestigious awards, including four honorary doctorates, in recognition of his contributions to leadership and organizational development.

THE MANAGEMENT OF LOSS

Humanity's Existential Crises

Manfred F. R. Kets de Vries

Routledge
Taylor & Francis Group
LONDON AND NEW YORK

Designed cover image: Getty Images – peych_p

First published 2026
by Routledge
4 Park Square, Milton Park, Abingdon, Oxon OX14 4RN

and by Routledge
605 Third Avenue, New York, NY 10158

Routledge is an imprint of the Taylor & Francis Group, an informa business

British Library Cataloguing-in-Publication Data
A catalogue record for this book is available from the British Library

ISBN: 978-1-041-09680-1 (hbk)
ISBN: 978-1-041-09030-4 (pbk)
ISBN: 978-1-003-65126-0 (ebk)

DOI: 10.4324/9781003651260

Typeset in Garamond
by Apex CoVantage, LLC

Contents

ABOUT THE AUTHOR

Manfred F. R. Kets de Vries brings a different view to the much-studied subjects of organizational dynamics, leadership, consulting, executive coaching, and psychotherapy. Bringing to bear his knowledge and experience of economics (Econ. Drs., University of Amsterdam), management (ITP, MBA, and DBA, Harvard Business School), and psychoanalysis (Membership Canadian Psychoanalytic Society, Paris Psychoanalytic Society, and the International Psychoanalytic Association), he explores individual and societal existential dilemmas in depth.

The Distinguished Clinical Professor of Leadership Development and Organizational Change at INSEAD, he is the founder of INSEAD's Executive Master Program in Change Management and has been the founder and former director of INSEAD's Global Leadership Centre. He has pioneered team coaching as an intervention method to help organizations and people change. As an educator, he has received INSEAD's Distinguished MBA Teacher Award six times and has held professorships at McGill University, HEC Montreal, and Harvard Business School. He is also a distinguished visiting professor at the European School for Management and Technology (ESMT), Berlin, and has lectured at management institutions around the world. *The Financial Times*, *Le Capital*, *Wirtschaftswoche*, and *The Economist* have rated Kets de Vries among the world's leading management thinkers and among the most influential contributors to human resource management.

Kets de Vries is the author, co-author, or editor of more than 60 books, including *The Neurotic Organization*; *Power and the Corporate Mind*; *Organizational Paradoxes*; *Struggling with the Demon: Perspectives on Individual and Organizational Irrationality*; *Handbook of Character Studies*; *The Irrational Executive*; *Leaders, Fools and Impostors*; *Life and Death in the Executive Fast Lane*; *Prisoners of Leadership*; *The Leadership Mystique*; *The Happiness Equation*; *Are Leaders Born or Are They Made? The Case of Alexander the Great*; *The New Russian Business Elite*; *Leadership by Terror: Finding Shaka Zulu in the Attic*; *The Leader on the Couch*; *Coach and Couch*; *The Family Business on the Couch*; *Sex, Money, Happiness, and Death: The Quest for Authenticity*; *Reflections on Leadership and Character*; *Reflections on Leadership and Career*; *Reflections on Organizations*; *The Coaching Kaleidoscope*; *The Hedgehog Effect: The Secrets of High Performance Teams*; *Mindful Leadership Coaching: Journeys into the Interior*; *You Will Meet a Tall Dark Stranger: Executive Coaching Challenges*; *Telling Fairy Tales in the Boardroom: How to Make Sure Your Organization Lives Happily*

Ever After; *Riding the Leadership Roller Coaster: A Psychological Observer's Guide*; *Down the Rabbit Hole of Leadership: Leadership Pathology of Everyday Life*; *The CEO Whisperer: Meditations on Leadership, Life and Change*; *Quo Vadis: The Existential Challenges of Leaders*; *Leadership Unhinged: Essays on the Ugly, the Bad, and the Weird*; *Leading Wisely: Becoming a Reflective Leader in Turbulent Times*; *The Daily Perils of Executive Life: How to Survive When Dancing on Quicksand*; *The Path to Authentic Leadership: Dancing with the Ouroboros*; *A Life Well Lived: Dialogues with a Kabouter*; *The Darker Side of Leadership: Pythons Devouring Crocodiles*; *Storytelling for Leaders: Tales of Sorrow and Love*; *Narcissistic Leadership: Narcissus on the Couch*; and *The Path to Individual and Organizational Transformation: Confronting the Elephant in the Room*. Furthermore, he has designed a number of 360-degree feedback instruments, including the widely used *Global Executive Leadership Mirror*, *Global Executive Leadership Inventory, Leadership Archetype Questionnaire, Internal Theatre Inventory*, and the *Organizational Culture Audit*.

In addition, he has published more than 400 academic papers as book chapters and articles and has also written more than 100 case studies, including seven that received the Best Case of the Year award. He has written hundreds of mini-articles (blogs) for the *Harvard Business Review, INSEAD Knowledge*, and other digital outlets, and is also a regular magazine contributor. His work has been featured in *The New York Times, The Wall Street Journal, The Los Angeles Times, Fortune, Business Week, The Economist, The Financial Times, The Straits Times, The New Statesman, The Harvard Business Review, Le Figaro, El País*, and *Het Financieele Dagblad*. His books and articles have been translated into more than 30 languages.

Professor Kets de Vries is a member of 17 editorial boards and is a Fellow of the Academy of Management. In addition, he is on the board of various charitable organizations and is also a founding member of the International Society for the Psychoanalytic Study of Organizations (ISPSO), which has honored him as a lifetime member. Kets de Vries is the first non-U.S. recipient of the International Leadership Association Lifetime Achievement Award for his contributions to leadership research and development. He has received a Lifetime Achievement Award from Germany for his advancement of executive education, and the American Psychological Association has honored him with the Harry and Miriam Levinson Award for his contributions to the field of organizational consultation. For his work advancing the interface between management and psychoanalysis, he is the recipient of the Freud Memorial Award. Furthermore, he has received the Vision of Excellence Award from the Harvard Institute of Coaching and is the first beneficiary of INSEAD's Dominique Héau Award for "Inspiring Educational Excellence." He has also been honored with four honorary doctorates, and the Dutch government has made him an Officer in the Order of Oranje Nassau.

Kets de Vries works as a consultant on organizational design, transformation, and strategic human resource management for companies worldwide. As an educator and consultant, he has worked in more than 40 countries. He is also the founder and non-executive chairman of the Kets de Vries Institute (KDVI), a boutique global strategic leadership development consulting firm with associates worldwide (www.kdvi.com).

On a more personal note, Kets de Vries was the first fly fisherman in Outer Mongolia (at the time becoming the world record holder of the Siberian *Hucho taimen* trout). He is a member of New York's Explorers Club and in his spare time he can be found in the rainforests or savannas of Central and Southern Africa, the Siberian taiga, the Ussuri Krai, the Kamchatka Peninsula, the Pamir and Altai Mountains, Arnhem Land, or within the Arctic Circle.

Website: www.kdvi.com

PREFACE

Had you even lost a friend, (which surely is the greatest of all losses) you ought rather to rejoice having had such a friend, than to mourn for having lost him.

—Seneca[1]

There is always after the death of anyone a kind of stupefaction; so difficult is it to grasp this advent of nothingness and to resign ourselves to believe in it.

—Gustave Flaubert[2]

My life, like the lives of all of us, was moved by unconscious forces which I did not really control and could only partly nudge in directions I may have consciously chosen at its various forks.

—Sudhir Kakar[3]

What prompted me to write this book about various types of loss was the death of my dear old friend Sudhir Kakar, sometimes called the father of Indian psychoanalysis. Although this moniker is impressive, Sudhir was much more than that. He was also a scholar in the fields of cultural psychology and the psychology of religion. As the eminent explorer of the Indian cultural psyche, he made sense of the country's religious, political, social, and erotic land-scapes. His book *The Inner World: A Psychoanalytic Study of Childhood and Society in India*[4] can be considered a prime example of this ability. I greatly admired too Sudhir's work as a novelist. He wrote several insightful novels addressing humanity's existential issues. Most importantly, he will be remembered for

DOI: 10.4324/9781003651260-1

his talent in bridging the Eastern and Western worlds, providing powerful insights into the universal human condition.

Apart from his remarkable scholarly contributions to intercultural psychoanalysis, Sudhir was a very good friend of mine. More than that, I always felt Sudhir was the older brother I never had. Our relationship began almost 60 years ago when we met at Harvard Business School during a seminar on psychoanalytic psychology and management theory given by my mentor Abraham Zaleznik.

At the time, I was a student in a special program of Harvard Business School, while Sudhir was a teaching fellow at Harvard University working with the well-known child psychoanalyst Erik Erikson. In his case, a chance encounter with Erikson—who was in India to research a biography on Gandhi—led to an invitation to become a teaching fellow at Harvard. The serendipitous encounter would transform my friend's life.

After the first seminar taught by Zaleznik, we discussed and compared notes. I remember that we conversed in German at the time. Feeling like kindred souls, we walked to Pamplona, a Harvard Square café, to talk about life, a conversation that began a life-long friendship. In fact, I have vivid memories of that first meeting, fascinated as I was by this warm-hearted, intellectually stimulating person who also possessed a great sense of humor.

> At the time, we couldn't have known that our connection would last a lifetime.

At the time, we couldn't have known that our connection would last a lifetime. I understood from our many conversations that he was set to become a management professor at the prestigious Indian Institute of Management (IIM) in Ahmedabad. At least, that was what his aunt—a professor at this institution—hoped would happen. Initially encouraged by his father to study engineering, he then studied business in Mannheim, Germany, before earning a doctorate in economics at the University of Vienna.

Despite Sudhir's reluctance to teach at a business school, he would be associated with IIM for some time, first as a member of the research staff, then as a faculty member in the field of organizational behavior. However, as was very clear from the beginning, his heart was not in business. Like his mentor Erikson, he wanted to become a psychoanalyst. Fortunately, years later he was offered the opportunity to study at the Sigmund Freud Institute in Frankfurt, where he would graduate as a psychoanalyst.

When Sudhir arrived in Frankfurt, I was living in France. As we hadn't seen each other for a while, I decided to visit him. My car broke down just before I arrived, so I had to climb through the snow up a hill to a somber, castle-like building where he was temporarily residing. His employer had provided this gloomy place as a temporary residence, which was filled with a collection of strange-looking Group Zero art. Assessing his situation, I realized that he was in for a tough period. His first wife struggled adjusting to the German environment, and the weather didn't help. However, despite these challenges, this period of exile turned out to be quite formative for him. Much later, we discussed the fact that when living in our own country, we tend to take its culture for granted. There are simply fewer opportunities to reflect on it. True reflections on culture only occur when we leave the place of our birth, either physically or mentally, and experience loss.

But let me go back to our time at Harvard. It was a pivotal period for both of us as we decided to become psychoanalysts, seeking deeper insights into the socio-cultural challenges facing society. In hindsight, I could not have predicted that Sudhir would become one of India's foremost cultural scholars. In his later writings and talks, he presented enriching global perspectives on the intricacies of cultural imagination and the mental representations of culture. To share his knowledge about societal issues, he became a visiting professor at many academic institutions, including Harvard, Chicago, McGill, Melbourne, Hawaii, and Vienna. He also served as a fellow at the Institutes of Advanced Study in Princeton, Berlin, and Cologne. In 2005, the French weekly *Le Nouvel Observateur* listed him as one of the world's 25 major thinkers, calling him "the psychoanalyst of civilizations."[5]

The book Sudhir produced during his stay at Harvard, a psychohistory of Frederick Taylor, the father of scientific management, foreshadowed his ability to be an astute observer of human nature. I also marveled at the way Sudhir combined psychoanalytic concepts with his deep knowledge of Indian myth, religion, culture, and society to produce extraordinarily insightful books about India and its people. He explored the influence of religion, social norms, and colonial legacies on intimate relationships and sexual expression. Sudhir truly knew how to decode the Indian psyche.

> True reflections on culture only occur when we leave the place of our birth, either physically or mentally, and experience loss.

After Boston—where we lived in a decrepit, cockroach-haunted building in the center of Harvard Square—we continued to meet in many places, particularly Vienna. We shared many happy moments visiting famous Viennese cafés or singing together at *Heurigen*, which are rustic wine taverns in Austria. To cement our friendship, I visited him many times in India. In fact, throughout my apartment, you'll find pictures of us together sitting on elephants or riding rickshaws. I also remember visiting his grand-uncle in Uttar Pradesh—a trip to the jungle that stayed with me. We also took a trip into the desert of Gujarat looking for wildlife and got lost.

I recall his parents very clearly. His father was a kind, quiet, somewhat avuncular man. In contrast, his mother was concerned with Sudhir's marital status, wishing that he would marry soon, which he was not ready to do. At the time, I realized how much his father had influenced Sudhir's interests. As a magistrate during British rule in India, his father frequently moved, exposing young Sudhir to a breadth of Indian cultures and the harrowing realities of partition. These experiences must have deeply influenced his understanding of the human psyche.

Much later, Sudhir spent a year at my house in Montreal while serving as a visiting professor at McGill University. I very much recall that he didn't enjoy the long winters. Every Saturday, to soothe his homesickness, our whole family would prepare a big Indian feast. During this time, he taught me a lot about Indian cooking, which I greatly enjoyed. After our Indian community lunch, Sudhir and I would often go and watch long Bollywood movies at events organized by the Indian community. We both loved the simplicity of the plots, with clear heroes and villains. I also remember how much we laughed while watching the film *The Party*,[6] where Peter Sellers plays a bungling Indian actor. Sudhir could handle a healthy dose of cultural self-criticism.

For more than 20 years, after I moved to Paris to teach at INSEAD, Sudhir became my collaborator in the top executive program "The Challenge of Leadership," which was centered around life case studies. As a good psychoanalyst, Sudhir wouldn't say much during these often emotional sessions, but when he did speak, people listened very carefully. I always marveled at his insights into the human condition. His contributions were formidable, not only for the students but also for me. Every comment was a great learning experience. These sessions also proved that Sudhir was a master storyteller. His ability to weave narratives around complex theories made his observations insightful and deeply engaging. Sudhir could bring lucidity and perspective to complex ideas, helping people understand their inner world and overcome their sense of loss.

Every comment was a great learning experience.

I also took great pleasure in seeing Sudhir hand out his translation of the *Kamasutra* in class. Obviously, this wasn't typical fare for a business school. The more astute students soon realized that this wasn't just a manual on sexual positions, but one of the oldest Hindu texts on the art of living. It gave them a glimpse into ancient Indian society, along with much advice on cultivating manners and the arts. The enigma of sexual desire has always been a topic very close to Sudhir's heart.

During these sessions, it became clear—central to Sudhir's work—just how valid and meaningful psychoanalysis, though originating in the West, could be within other cultural contexts. However, Sudhir would emphasize the differences between psychoanalysis based on Judeo-Christian ideas and one founded on a Hindu imagination. He also highlighted the importance of community orientation over individual orientation, a concept relevant not only to Indian culture but also common to many Asian civilizations: interdependence versus independence. In emphasizing the differences, he would also make us reflect on the dark side of both visions. While that of individualism is unbridled selfishness and greed, the dark side of communitarianism is its intolerance and potential for violence. Sudhir would point out that most of our knowledge about how humans feel, think, and act is derived from a small subset described as WEIRD—Western, educated, industrialized, rich, and democratic.

But enough theoretical musings. One day, Sudhir learned that he had cancer. I remember his wife Katha saying, "Together we will overcome." Cancer treatment is always an ordeal, but I can't imagine what it must have been for someone who had never been hospitalized before. With Katha's heroic help, he survived this awful period, though he was much weakened.

While the dark side of individualism is unbridled selfishness and greed, the dark side of communitarianism is its intolerance and potential for violence.

Sudhir must have sensed he had limited time left, as he decided to visit Europe one more time for old times' sake. When I met him, he was a shadow of his former self—a man who once had a commanding presence and a shock of thick, curly hair. However, he remained sharp. With Katha, he stayed at my apartment in the center of Paris. Every evening, continuing an old tradition, we went to a café on my street. This time, the vodka and cigars were absent, but the wine remained. We reminisced about old times, and once more, I was reminded of his remarkable intellect and keen ability to observe people. Sudhir was always a man of great contrasts; when he wanted, he could be quite charming, but at heart, he was quite a shy person.

Soon after that week in Paris, knowing that time was running out, I decided to visit him in Goa with my youngest daughter. I sensed it would be the last time. In fact, both of us knew that this was the case, but we didn't talk about it. As before, I participated in his evening ritual of going for a drink at the beach, a ten-minute drive from his traditional home in Benaulim, South Goa. This last time—gazing at the sea together—is a memory that will stay with me. I get very emotional looking at the picture of the two of us standing on his veranda, knowing it would be our last goodbye.

> Grief is the price we pay for feeling very close to someone. No matter how prepared we think we are for the death of a loved one, it still comes as a shock and hurts deeply.

When Katha told me that the end was near, I went into a state of shock. I know that death awaits us all, but it was hard to accept that he would no longer be there, that we could no longer joke together, and that I could no longer enjoy his insights about the human condition. His passing left me with a deep sense of loss. It felt like I had fallen into a void. This brings home the truth that grief is the price we pay for feeling very close to someone. No matter how prepared we think we are for the death of a loved one, it still comes as a shock and hurts deeply. The sadness will never disappear.

Sudhir left a footprint that won't fade. Apart from his significant contributions to cultural psychoanalysis, Sudhir was also what the Germans call a *Lebenskünstler*, literally translated as a life artist—one who lives life to the fullest. Fortunately, he shared many of his happy moments with me.

> When addressing the theme of loss, death always surfaces. A key thing is that death should not prevent people from living.

In dealing with life's challenges, I have found writing to be a good remedy. To process my feelings regarding Sudhir's passing, I decided to write on the subject of loss, which happened to be a regular theme in the seminars we ran together. These losses could be varied, both work-related and personal. Naturally, in my profession, I deal with many kinds of work-related losses. But when addressing the theme of loss, death always surfaces. A key thing is that death should not prevent people from living. As the Roman emperor Marcus Aurelius once said, "If your fear is not that you will cease to live, but that you never started a life in accordance with nature [growth and flourishing], then you will be a man worthy of the universe that gave you birth."[7] I believe that people who live life to the fullest don't fear death. As a *Lebenskünstler*, Sudhir understood that death is not the opposite of life but a part of it. It is all part of being human. This didn't make our last goodbyes any easier.

Hindu cultural heritage sees life not only as a tragedy but also as a romantic quest spanning many lifetimes, with the goal of reaching a higher level of reality beyond the empirical world we live in.

In Hinduism, Shiva represents transformation. Through destruction and restoration, this deity reminds us that endings are beginnings, and that our world is constantly undergoing a cycle of birth, death, and rebirth. All this would have resonated with Sudhir and his Indian imagination. He might have viewed death as a form of union as much as it is a moment of separation. In that respect, the Hindu cultural heritage sees life not only as a tragedy but also as a romantic quest spanning many lifetimes, with the goal of reaching a higher level of reality beyond the empirical world we live in.

Odd as it may sound, this book is my way of revisiting Sudhir's legacy as a cultural critic and pioneer of intercultural psychoanalysis. A brilliant writer, he challenged traditional perspectives and deepened our understanding of the human experience. But foremost, this book celebrates an old friendship. After all, friendships make life bearable. Sudhir accepted me for who I am and helped me become who I should be. As the Alsatian humanitarian Albert Schweitzer once said, "Often our light goes out but is blown again into flame by an encounter with another human being. Each of us owes the deepest thanks to those who have rekindled this inner light."[8]

Friendships make life bearable.

NOTES

1   Lucius Annæus Seneca (1786/c. 65 AD). *The Epistles of Lucius Annæus Seneca*. Trans. and ed. Thomas Morell. London: W. Woodfall, Volume II, Letter XCIX.
2   Gustave Flaubert (1886/1857). *Madame Bovary*. Trans. Eleanor Marx-Aveling. London: Vizetelly & Co.
3   Sudhir Kakar was a close personal friend of Professor Kets de Vries; this is reproduced with permission from his family.
4   Sudhir Kakar (2012/1978). *The Inner World: A Psychoanalytical Study of Childhood and Society in India* (4th edn). Oxford: Oxford University Press.
5   https://ipaoffthecouch.org/2024/05/05/episode-158-an-analysts-hindu-indian-imagination-with-sudhir-kakar-goa-india

6 *The Party* (1968). Dir. Blake Edwards. United Artists.

7 Marcus Aurelius (2006/170–180 AD). *Meditations*. Trans. with notes Martin Hammond. Harmondsworth, UK: Penguin, Book 12.

8 Albert Schweitzer. Cited in Erica Anderson (1956). *The World of Albert Schweitzer: A Book of Photographs*. New York: Harper & Bros.

INTRODUCTION

Everything that has a beginning has an ending. Make your peace with that and all will be well.

—Buddhist saying

Make the most of your regrets; never smother your sorrow, but tend and cherish it till it comes to have a separate and integral interest. To regret deeply is to live afresh.

—Henry David Thoreau[1]

During our lifetime, we will experience many losses affecting our internal and external worlds. Difficult as these various losses may be, we should realize that they are an inevitable part of life. Like it or not, loss is part of the human condition. Life goes on. Losses can also be seen as growth experiences. Every time we hurt, we should pay attention, as life may be trying to tell us something. As the German philosopher Arthur Schopenhauer noted, "Mostly it is loss which teaches us about the worth of things."[2]

Like it or not, loss is part of the human condition.
Life goes on.

Sure enough, each of the losses I have experienced led to personal insights that I wouldn't have had otherwise. But it's also clear to me that loss doesn't always lead to growth. Some people diminish after suffering loss; they break

DOI: 10.4324/9781003651260-2

down or get stuck in the grieving process. Some even experience serious stress symptoms as a result of their loss.

Clearly, loss isn't something that can be avoided. It is a natural aspect of the rhythm of life. Still, coping with grief will always be a challenge. As I mentioned in the preface to this book, the most profound loss is that of those closest to us.

Loss can manifest itself in many more ways than death-related grief. For example, some losses pertain to our inner architecture and can affect our life's journey. We may not even realize that we are experiencing a loss in our ability to test reality, as unconscious processes influence how we deal with life's challenges. We don't fully understand our actions; "we are at a loss."

Estrangement is another type of loss involving many conscious and unconscious processes. Clearly, in cases of divorce or separation, or when an important friendship ends, we experience strong feelings of loss. We grieve the loss of the relationship, which may even affect our sense of self and challenge our feelings of security—the confidence we had in the predictability of life. If so, it can take some time to adjust to our new external landscape.

In the context of work, being let go or quitting can bring a great sense of loss. Leaving a job is always challenging. Also, we may experience loss when we reach retirement. If so, aside from possible financial worries creating insecurity, we may also lose our sense of identity if our job or career was a key part of how we viewed ourselves.

From a mental health and healing perspective, it is better to acknowledge the loss and allow ourselves to feel the emotions that emerge, painful as they may be.

We must pay attention to the emotions that arise due to loss. Are we prepared to express our emotions or are we keeping them in check? From a mental health and healing perspective, it is better to acknowledge the loss and allow ourselves to feel the emotions that emerge, painful as they may be.

Naturally, our cultural background influences how we understand and approach the experience of loss. Each culture has different ways of dealing with this matter. For example, some cultures have developed elaborate mourning rituals to help people work through their sense of loss. These rituals and ceremonies help people acknowledge the pain of loss while offering social support and a reaffirmation of life. In other cultures, however, this may not be the case. People are expected to behave stoically, remain calm, and show almost no emotions, acting as if everything is fine. In such cultures, little or no social support or empathy is expected from others.

Consequently, certain losses may not be visible to others, even though they may have taken the central stage in a person's inner life.

Sudden, unexpected loss can exceed our coping abilities,
leaving us feeling overwhelmed and unable to function.

Apart from the cultural dimension, there are other ways to differentiate loss. For example, sudden, unexpected loss can exceed our coping abilities, leaving us feeling overwhelmed and unable to function. Then there is the form of loss that allows for anticipatory mourning. This type of loss can be considered a natural process, enabling the person to prepare gradually for the reality of what is about to happen. Finally, there is traumatic loss due to natural disasters, such as hurricanes, tsunamis, and earthquakes, as well as human-made mass shootings.

When coping with loss, we might be so overwhelmed with emotions that we can't think clearly. Images associated with our loss may haunt us at any time. Certain kinds of losses can make life seem meaningless, unjust, and unpredictable, leaving us feeling stuck in the grieving process. Anxiety attacks and feelings of depression, among other reactions, may persist over long periods of time. Complicated grief doesn't necessarily subside on its own. While time may heal some losses, it may also create new ones.

Complicated grief doesn't necessarily subside on its own.

As I dealt with the passing of my friend Sudhir, I realized that, over the years, I had written several essays on the topic of loss. In this book, I have expanded on this material, exploring this subject from various angles, often using a psychodynamic-systemic lens. When appropriate, I've also applied concepts from developmental psychology, neuroscience, and evolutionary psychology. In addition, I've included case examples of people, encountered in my work, who have navigated various kinds of losses. Given that much of my work as an academic, consultant, coach, and psychotherapist takes place in the professional sphere, it's no surprise that many of the case examples in these essays are set in managerial contexts.

By means of psychodynamic-systemic and neurological perspectives, the first essay illustrates that we should let go of the illusion that we are in control of our lives. We like to believe that we are logical thinkers, but the reality is quite different. We aren't truly rational actors, although if we make the effort, we may discover a rationale behind our seemingly irrational behavior. The conflict between good intentions and actions, influenced by unconscious processes, can contribute to a sense of loss. It makes us realize that full control eludes us—a fact that many people find disturbing.

We should let go of the illusion that
we are in control of our lives.

The next two essays are very much work-related. The first concerns job loss resulting from the behavior of a person's superiors. I'm referring to poor leadership practices, such as micromanagement, bullying, conflict avoidance, and narcissistic behavior. The second essay focuses on the sense of loss some people experience due to retirement. While retirement can be seen as a reward for years of hard work, it can also trigger various stress symptoms.

The essay that follows is of a very different nature. It deals with how our imagination can go wild, allowing unconscious fears to haunt us. It discusses the bogeyman represented by artificial intelligence (AI). Many people are concerned that AI may take control of the world as we know it. However, this fear represents another kind of loss: the fear that, sooner or later, we will no longer fit into present-day society and that our capabilities will become irrelevant.

Given the importance of feeling alive—a state of being so fully immersed in what we're doing that we lose ourselves in it—the next three essays concern another form of loss: the loss of interest in life, or boredom. When people experience this, nothing is of interest to them. They are at a loss for what can give them pleasure. Having lost their zest for life, these people are unsure how to continue. Unfortunately, these feelings of loss may contribute to self-destructive behaviors. In these essays, however, I also suggest that boredom shouldn't be viewed purely negatively. It can also be a warning sign, telling us that it's time to explore new avenues. Furthermore, I observe that in today's overly entertained society, boredom may have become more prevalent, reaching pandemic proportions in some demographics.

In today's overly entertained society, boredom may have
become more prevalent, reaching pandemic proportions in
some demographics.

The essays that follow focus on another form of loss: feelings of loneliness or the loss of companionship. As social creatures, human beings need positive interpersonal relationships for greater overall life satisfaction. Social connection is a basic human necessity, providing a sense of safety, hope, and belonging. When there is a breakdown in interpersonal relationships, people may begin to experience deficits in both psychological and physical well-being. They're losing out on life.

The subsequent two essays address another form of loss: the loss of the ability to have intimate relationships due to sexual addiction. While sex is an essential human need, to make the experience meaningful it needs to be combined with feelings of intimacy and care. For some people, however, difficulties in dealing with intimate relationships have caused sexuality to take on an obsessive quality. In these essays, I suggest that using sex purely for hedonistic pleasure may not be beneficial for mental health. It becomes a way of masking other issues one refuses to deal with. "Manic" sexual acrobatics then serve as a compensatory activity, covering a deep sense of loss. Engaging in these acts of escape can reduce people's self-awareness and prevent them from leading a well-rounded life.

While sex is an essential human need, to make the experience meaningful it needs to be combined with feelings of intimacy and care.

The next essay deals with another form of loss: the experience of physical symptoms that, in the mind of the sufferer, appear to have gotten out of control, as in the case of hypochondria. Affected people are confused about what's going on with their body. Their intense thoughts, feelings, and behaviors related to the symptoms leave them at a loss for how to cope with life's vicissitudes.

Next come three essays focused on the most dramatic form of loss: death. As I made clear in the preface to this book, coping with the loss of someone we are very close to is one of life's greatest challenges. These essays begin with an exploration of manic work behavior, which can be interpreted as a way of warding off death anxiety. People prone to workaholism experience a serious loss: they aren't truly living. Many workaholics use incessant activity to keep depressive thoughts at bay, pushing away a lingering, out-of-awareness fear of death. In this context, I also discuss the compulsion to deny death. Here, I highlight "immortality systems"—imaginary ways of continuing life to cope with this ultimate form of loss. Furthermore, I address grief and mourning; in other words, the feelings and behaviors following the loss of people who mattered to us. Apart from distinguishing these two experiences, I note that grieving the loss of loved ones may turn into a never-ending process. However, it can also be the catalyst for a renewed sense of meaning, offering purpose and direction to life.

> Many workaholics use incessant activity to keep depressive thoughts at bay, pushing away a lingering, out-of-awareness fear of death.

The final essay focuses on the interchange between philosophers and psychologists. I observe that in dealing with existential crises pertaining to loss, it helps to understand both psychology and philosophy. For some philosophers, the theme of emotional and mental distress has always been at the top of their minds—a theme also close to those in the helping professions. Both fields have always dealt with the ultimate concerns of humankind, such as death, freedom, isolation, and meaninglessness. In that respect, I suggest that existentially oriented psychological interventions can be quite effective, as they integrate philosophical insights with therapeutic practices to address essential human dilemmas.

> In dealing with existential crises pertaining to loss, it helps to understand both psychology and philosophy.

In all these essays, when appropriate, I address ways of dealing with these various losses. As mental health includes emotional, psychological, and social well-being, my recommendations range from self-help activities to reaching out to a helping professional. I also emphasize that self-care and self-compassion are crucial to safeguard our well-being and cope with daily stressors.

As I try to make clear in this book, dealing with loss of any kind will always be a challenging process that affects us in different ways. But it is an experience that none of us can escape. Consequently, when we feel low due to loss, we should not view it as a disorder or a sign of weakness. On the contrary, it demonstrates that we are only human.

> Self-care and self-compassion are crucial to safeguard our well-being and cope with daily stressors.

Let me end this introduction by saying that loss is like a moving river, an ever-changing experience. As the Persian poet Rúmí once said, "Anything you lose comes round in another form."[3] Grieving our losses is part of humanity's rites of passage. In fact, the ability to grieve whenever we experience a loss can be seen as an emotional, physical, and spiritual necessity. Although challenging, it is a form of self-care. When we are faced with loss, grief seems to have a beginning but no end. Only its shape tends to change. At the same time, strange as it may seem, life still goes on. Somehow, the world keeps on turning. Given that this is life's reality, we would be wise to heed an old Chinese proverb: "You cannot prevent the birds of sorrow from flying over your head, but you can prevent them from building nests in your hair."

When we are faced with loss, grief seems to have a beginning but no end. Only its shape tends to change.

NOTES

1 Henry David Thoreau (1906/1839). Entry of 13 November 1839. In *The Writings of Henry David Thoreau in 20 Volumes*. Ed. Bradford Torrey. Boston, MA: Houghton Mifflin, Vol. VII.

2 Originally: *Meistens belehrt erst der Verlust uns über den Werth der Dinge*. https://d-nb.info/1041219032/34, p. 128. Author's translation.

3 Jalálu'ddín Rúmí (1999/c. 1258 ff). Unmarked Boxes. In *Rumi: Selected Poems*. Trans. Coleman Banks with John Moyne, A.J. Arberry, and Reynold Nicholson. Harmondsworth, UK: Penguin.

1

WHY ARE WE FOOLING OURSELVES?

Hell is paved with good intentions.

—Samuel Johnson[1]

Properly speaking, the unconscious is the real psychic; its inner nature is just as unknown to us as the reality of the external world, and it is just as imperfectly reported to us through the data of consciousness as is the external world through the indications of our sensory organs.

—Sigmund Freud[2]

As suggested, this book of essays explores many kinds of loss. Of course, the most significant kind of loss concerns death. However, as previously mentioned, there are many other experiences that can contribute to a sense of loss. An important one is the realization that human beings aren't rational actors—while there may be a logic behind our actions, they do not always appear rational. *Homo rationalis*, the prototype of the economic man who is assumed to be perfectly rational with an infinite ability to make sound decisions, is a myth. Still, we cling to this mythological figure because it is difficult to accept that we aren't in full control of our lives and that we're often at a loss to understand why we do what we do.

There are many experiences that contribute to a sense of loss. One is the realization that human beings aren't rational actors—while there may be a logic behind our actions, they do not always appear rational.

DOI: 10.4324/9781003651260-3

For example, take work. As a leader of an organization, have you become ineffective? Are you a perfectionist? Are you a procrastinator? Are you conflict-avoidant? Do you suffer from analysis paralysis? Are you a leader in orbit, too distant from everyone? Do you steamroll your people? Have you become over-judgmental? In other words, reflecting on these leadership scenarios, do you possess certain behavior patterns that make you rather dysfunctional?

Many of these behavior patterns are commonly observed. What's less obvious is whether you *realize* you are behaving in this manner—that you're acting dysfunctionally. Do you recognize that this may be the case? And if so, do you want to do something about it? Still, though you realize that something is wrong, are you at a loss as to why this is happening to you? Could it be that you lack intrapsychic control?

Of course, you may have every intention to change your behavior once you discover that you're behaving ineffectually. But as we all know, good intentions alone are not enough. Even if you realize you have a problem, doing something about it is another matter. There may be a gap between your good intentions and your actions, between what you say you plan to do and what you're actually doing. You might ask yourself if it has to be this way. If you realize that your behavior has become dysfunctional, why do you seem unable to take remedial action? What's holding you back? Why are you at a loss for what to do about your situation?

Frequently, there is a split between what we think we're doing and what we're really doing. If that's the case, we are stuck.

THE POWER OF THE UNCONSCIOUS

The fact is that we may be quite unaware of why we do what we do. Frequently, there is a split between what we think we're doing and what we're really doing. If that's the case, we are stuck. We aren't on a personal growth trajectory, and we aren't making the best of our abilities. The question then becomes: Why are we stuck? Why is there a gap between what we say we will do and what we do?

Out-of-awareness behavior significantly influences our likes and dislikes, our judgments, our abilities, and our potential.

We must accept that it isn't always easy to align our actual behavior with our good intentions. The reason for this divergence is the power of our unconscious. Many unconscious psychological dynamics influence the way we make decisions.

Often, we are at a loss to understand why this is the case. Whatever the reasons, we must accept that out-of-awareness behavior significantly influences our likes and dislikes, our judgments, our abilities, and our potential. Due to these unconscious dynamics, we are often unable to view ourselves accurately. To add insult to injury, we are not very accurate when judging how others see us.

It is always hard to accept that we aren't in full control of our lives—that an unconscious, less reflective, and more emotional part of our mind influences our decisions. To understand why this is the case, we need to explore our brain. From a neurological perspective, there is tension between the prefrontal cortex, known for its logical and analytical orientation, and the amygdala, which mediates many aspects of emotion and memory. The amygdala plays a key role in stressful situations, often overriding the prefrontal cortex's more logical approach to decision-making. This can trigger a fight-or-flight response. Consequently, this tension makes us appear to act illogically. While we may be at a loss to understand our actions, our behavior has a rationale that is beyond our immediate conscious awareness. It becomes clear that our unconscious has its own logic. If we try to figure out why we do what we do, we might be quite surprised by what we find. It can be a real eye-opener.

> It is always hard to accept that we aren't in full control of our lives—that an unconscious, less reflective, and more emotional part of our mind influences our decisions.

Even if we accept that we're influenced by these neurological processes, we don't like to be told that many of our decisions are not grounded in traditional logic and reason, and that much of our judgment and behavior is produced with very little conscious thought. However, if we look closely, we will discover that almost all of our brain's activity occurs below the level of consciousness. Of course, many of these unconscious processes involve the monitoring of our body's vital functions—from controlling breathing to processing incoming information.

> Our unconscious has its own logic.

Still, realizing that we aren't completely in control of our actions is unsettling. We fear losing control over our life and the power of choice. This fear creates a feeling of losing out in life. We like to hold on to the illusion that our behavior is guided by conscious, rational thought. However, there will be occasions when it appears we are acting against our own best interests—an unconscious "sabotage."

At times, the way we think versus the way we act makes it seem as if our brain is split. We may decide one thing consciously, but our unconscious seems to have a completely different agenda. As a result, things don't turn out as we had planned. However, we need to realize that conscious reasoning constitutes only a small part of our brain's activities, with most work occurring in places that are not easily reachable. It has been estimated that as much as 90–95 percent of our behavior and decisions derive from the unconscious.[3] Therefore, there is a very good chance that our "rational" intentions may be derailed.

Feelings should be interpreted as warning signs. Like traffic lights, these flashing yellow lights that are our feelings tell us to slow down, review our surroundings, and then decide what to do.

In fact, we often seem to be strangers to ourselves, possessed by a highly sophisticated unconscious mind that operates in parallel to our conscious mind and that may interpret the world very differently than we consciously think.[4] This doesn't mean we are completely unaware of what we're doing or have no room to maneuver. There are many aspects of our life that we can control. For example, we do experience our feelings. We *know* when we feel glad, mad, sad, or bad. We *know* when we feel disgusted. These feelings should be interpreted as warning signs. Like traffic lights, these flashing yellow lights that are our feelings tell us to slow down, review our surroundings, and then decide what to do. Each indicator can be used as an important signal to alert us that our emotional heat is rising and needs our attention. What causes these emotional reactions, however, is not always very clear. Yet, becoming aware of these emotions is essential for learning to respond deliberately, rather than reacting impulsively in ways that sabotage our best efforts.

Sigmund Freud, in his seminal essay *New Introductory Lectures on Psychoanalysis*, explained the gap between good intentions and reality using the metaphor of the rider and the horse. The illustration highlights the endless conflict between emotional impulses and the forces of reason. In Freud's metaphor, the horse represents the source of our basic emotional impulses (the id), while the rider represents our reason (the ego). According to him:

One might compare the relation of the ego to the id with that between a rider and his horse. The horse provides the locomotor energy, and the rider has the prerogative of determining the goal and of guiding the movements of his powerful mount towards it. But all too often in the relations between the ego and the id we find a picture of the less ideal situation in which the rider is obliged to guide his horse in the direction in which it itself wants to go.[5]

How we manage to resolve this conflict between reason and emotion determines our behavior and actions.

Basically, Freud was referring to how we manage our character—the way we think, feel, and behave—which distinguishes us from others. It also addresses the question of how to manage our character to maintain our psychological equilibrium. This is not always easy. Deep down, human beings tend to be quite anxious. Given our evolutionary heritage, when many life-threatening dangers were ever-present, we remain constantly besieged by a plethora of anxieties that haunt us both consciously and unconsciously.

But are we aware of these anxieties? Moreover, do we know how to address them? To speak truthfully, not really. In fact, many of these concerns remain unconscious. Our concerns are often expressed through our feelings. Therefore, we often do what we *feel* like doing. Contemporary neuroscience suggests that our feelings drive much of our behavior, logical thinking be damned. So much for *Homo economicus.*

Deep down, human beings tend to be quite anxious. Given our evolutionary heritage, when many life-threatening dangers were ever-present, we remain constantly besieged by a plethora of anxieties that haunt us both consciously and unconsciously.

RIDING THE ELEPHANT

To understand better what I am referring to, it may be useful to replace Freud's horse metaphor with that of an elephant. This metaphor might help us make sense of what makes us "tick" and understand the processes that occur beneath the surface. What are the basic forces that determine our character?

Anyone who has ever ridden an elephant knows that steering it can be very challenging. To do so effectively requires a deep understanding of how it functions. The rider needs to know the elephant's peculiarities. For starters, changing course while sitting on an elephant presents its own difficulties. Frankly speaking, the elephant is somewhat lazy. It doesn't really like to change and prefers the status quo. This should serve as a warning to those who believe in instant change—who think that it is easy to change our behavior. Naturally, people in the helping professions know better. And many of us have learned the hard way that changing a person's behavior can be an uphill struggle. Often, we find ourselves at a total loss trying to change behavior patterns. It is very hard work. The armor that is character can be hard to crack!

> Often, helping professionals find themselves at a total
> loss trying to change behavior patterns. It is very hard
> work. The armor that is character can be hard to crack!

Furthermore, we should add that the elephant is somewhat paranoid. This attitude—this way of looking at the world—is probably also a remnant of our evolutionary heritage. Given the many dangers our Paleolithic ancestors faced, it was essential to be always on guard. A non-stop anxiety that something awful was about to happen was warranted. The expression "only the paranoid survive" rings true here. What's more, when bad things happen, the elephant quickly takes offense. Tit-for-tat tends to be its natural reaction. The elephant is very much inclined toward retaliation—to get even. It follows the code of reciprocal justice, subscribing to the ancient Babylonian law of "an eye for an eye."

Most importantly, however, the elephant is quite narcissistic. Deep down, the elephant perceives itself as quite special and is very self-seeking. Given this outlook, we tend to see ourselves much more positively than others do. As the elephant is continually preoccupied with its self-worth, everything that happens is interpreted in a highly egocentric manner. This strong feeling of self-love is likely needed to protect us against the many setbacks of life. But, as we are all too aware, life is not a rose garden. Disease and death are inevitable parts of life. Consequently, self-love helps in maintaining our psychological equilibrium. It makes us more stress-resistant. From an evolutionary perspective, this inflated sense of self is beneficial and, in some respects, necessary.

> From an evolutionary perspective, our inflated sense
> of self is beneficial and, in some respects, necessary.

The implication of this behavior pattern is that, to maintain its mental equilibrium, the elephant needs a continuous narcissistic supply. It constantly requires others to provide recognition to sustain its self-esteem. No wonder the elephant's self-views tend to be exaggerated. No wonder it is so full of itself. From an evolutionary and biological perspective, this narcissism may have contributed to its survival and the perpetuation of the species. Such behavior likely has a reproductive payoff.

Returning to the elephant's inherent narcissistic makeup, it is constantly driven to prove its worth, not only to others but also to itself. From a self-regulatory viewpoint, to maintain its mental health, the elephant must strive to feel and appear positive, special, successful, and important. The elephant has become an expert in complimenting itself. However, this need for a continuous narcissistic supply indicates that the elephant's self-esteem can easily be deflated. The elephant isn't as self-assured as it may seem. Given its psychological fragility, the elephant finds it difficult to acknowledge any criticism of itself. This explains its elaborate defense system to ward off any sign of weakness. It is why the elephant has such a hard time admitting real vulnerability, deficiency, or culpability. Admitting any weakness or imperfection too easily creates feelings of inferiority.

Therefore, when the elephant feels threatened by criticism, it is very talented at turning things around. It is a master at deflecting faultfinding. It is quick to blame others for any shortcomings, or, if necessary, to falsify (not necessarily consciously) any evidence of its deficiencies. The elephant has many other ways of deflecting criticism, such as changing the subject or responding as though it has been asked something entirely different.

We are all programmed with a deeply self-serving bias. This means we tend to overestimate our contributions to our successes and, in case of failure, blame others or attribute it to forces beyond our control.

Substituting the elephant once more for our character, we are all programmed with a deeply self-serving bias. This means we tend to overestimate our contributions to our successes and, in case of failure, blame others or attribute it to forces beyond our control. This kind of positive reframing is important, as it helps maintain our mental equilibrium. It lets us avoid feelings of depression and maintain the self-esteem, confidence, and optimism needed to keep going. This explains why our internal theater's main themes (most of them occurring out of our awareness) involve *attempts at avoiding vulnerability* and the *need for approval* in whatever we do. Thus, in understanding our behavior, we must always remind ourselves that the elephant has very thin skin. The elephant inside us will fight anything that appears to be a threat to its mental equilibrium, through processes that take place beyond conscious awareness.

The point I am trying to make is that the dominance of unconscious processes stems from the fact that the elephant within is *always* in survival mode, both physically and mentally. Although we may express our rational thoughts, a compelling need to satisfy the narcissistic needs of our inner elephant lurks in the shadows. This constant sense of vulnerability isn't something we are fully aware of, nor is it something we like to talk about. Even though we may be at a loss to understand why we do what we do, this concern will always be present.

> Although we may express our rational thoughts,
> a compelling need to satisfy the narcissistic
> needs of our inner elephant lurks in the shadows.

The powerful force of the elephant inside us makes us act both consistently and inconsistently. It is the reason that we are often unaware of the contradiction between what we say we do and what we really do—between how we think we're acting and how we actually act. We may be puzzled why this happens. We act the way we do to protect ourselves from the fear of embarrassment and feelings of vulnerability or incompetence. Thus, most of the time, our conflicting behavior should be seen as a result of this contradiction. It creates a gap between good intentions and reality.

> We are often unaware of the contradiction between
> what we say we do and what we really do—between
> how we think we're acting and how we actually act.

THE ELEPHANT IN THE CHINA SHOP OF ORGANIZATIONS

Now, let's place the elephant in a managerial setting. One important example from the professional sphere is why so many executives look at the world through perfectionistic glasses. Why do some of them feel compelled to be so controlling? Why can't they let go? What makes it so difficult for certain executives to empower others? From a rational point of view, this behavior doesn't make sense. It leads to micromanagement and a reluctance to delegate. Furthermore, even when these individuals recognize that micromanagement is ineffective, they seem resistant to change. Often, they have received feedback for years that micromanaging is not effective and that they should find better ways to deal with their teams. These executives always promise to change, yet nothing happens despite their good intentions. They fail to delegate, they don't allow for small failures, and they don't let their people take charge. Why this gap?

What's really going on is that these people don't know how to manage the elephant inside. They don't realize that the elephant's narcissistic, unconscious strivings override their conscious good intentions. As a result, they have no control over their intrapsychic life. These individuals may say all the right things but continue to do all the wrong things. They seem unable to help themselves. Something compels them to revert to unconscious behavior. They remain preoccupied with avoiding vulnerability and missing the kudos they need to fuel their self-esteem. Thus the gap just mentioned. They end up with confused goals, feeling stuck, and unable to understand why this is happening to them.

> Most models of human behavior are built on the faulty premise that
> we make decisions by consciously weighing all the relevant factors.

What I am trying to illustrate with the elephant metaphor is that most models of human behavior are built on the faulty premise that we make decisions by *consciously* weighing all the relevant factors. It is assumed that we *consciously* decide on the best option and subsequently make a conscious decision. However, as contemporary brain research points out[6]—seeing the elephant at work—this is not usually the case. Instead, we often act based on simple, unconscious rules that can produce seemingly irrational results. These actions, however, have a rationale when we consider the forces of the unconscious.

CLOSING THE GAP

The million-dollar question becomes: How do we become more aware of this out-of-awareness behavior? What can we do to tame the elephant? How can we outsmart the unconscious processes of the brain? To do so, we need to find ways to evaluate honestly what we really do. We need to create a psychological space that allows us to reflect on our behavior and develop a desire to change it if it proves ineffective.

But how can we use our reflective, analytical mind to devise ways to override some of the unconscious processes that create this gap between what we say we do and what we actually do? Given the elephant's reluctance to change, this is not going to be a walk in the park.

> The good news is that although the unconscious contains powerful
> forces that can derail good intentions, it can still be overruled.

The good news is that although the unconscious contains powerful forces that can derail good intentions, it can still be overruled. The reflective, conscious part of our brain is not without its own power. We are not on automatic pilot; we have some wiggle room. Most of us possess the ability to observe ourselves and use these observations to guide conscious action. Through reflection, we can attain greater control over what we do and narrow the gap between our good intentions and reality. But to make this happen, we must deconstruct unconscious processes and closely examine what is happening to us.

In deconstructing our unconscious, it is helpful to remember that it operates through emotions and symbols. Furthermore, it serves as a storage facility for our memories, which are organized in different ways depending on how we feel. Some memories evoke good feelings, whereas others have the opposite effect. Let's keep in mind that feelings are major drivers of behavior. The associations related to these feelings can become conscious, or the brain may prefer to keep them unconscious. Thus, in our brains there is a constant interplay between conscious and unconscious processes. To maintain our psychic equilibrium, the brain may hide certain memories (such as traumas) associated with strong negative emotions until we are prepared to process them consciously. Due to this interplay between conscious and unconscious associations, the elephant is constantly on guard, striving to protect its mental equilibrium and showing little sympathy for negative feedback.

> If we want to understand better why we act the way we do,
> we need to be somewhat vulnerable. Here, it helps when
> we don't delude ourselves into thinking that we are perfect.

If we want to understand better why we act the way we do, we need to be somewhat vulnerable. Here, it helps when we don't delude ourselves into thinking that we are perfect. We need to recognize the gap between what we say we do and what we *really* do. Also, we must have a desire to improve and be willing to step outside our comfort zones. Furthermore, it helps when we can listen to feedback and hear constructive criticism without becoming defensive. We also need to cope with the sense of loss we may experience when we realize the difference between our fantasies and reality.

When embarking on a journey towards change, we should thus be prepared to address uncomfortable topics. We should be ready to reflect on our behavior and analyze how it affects others. We should also be able to process the feedback given to us. Doing all these things requires at least a modest amount of self-awareness and self-knowledge.

> We need to cope with the sense of loss we may experience when we
> realize the difference between our fantasies and reality.

Self-awareness means perceiving, knowing, and being conscious of our thoughts, behaviors, emotions, beliefs, and sensory experiences. By developing self-awareness, we can better understand our own behaviors, emotions, beliefs, and values in interpersonal and group encounters. Essentially, self-awareness refers to a real-time understanding of our emotional and mental states. In comparison, self-knowledge is the understanding acquired through experience, revealing what we are truly about. It means being aware of our strengths and weaknesses, as well as the intricate motivations, desires, and fears that drive us. It involves delving deeply into our unconscious, peeling back the layers to reveal the core of our identity.

Self-knowledge involves delving deeply into our unconscious, peeling back the layers to reveal the core of our identity.

RECEIVING FEEDBACK

One insight that may help us be more receptive to feedback is the realization that we often see things in others that they don't see in themselves. We may recognize behavior patterns in other people of which they are completely unaware. We may see things that block them from being more effective and find it puzzling that they have these blind spots. However, this insight into others can also be turned around. Other people may have the same impression of us. They may be puzzled as to why we don't see our own dysfunctional behavior, why we are at a loss, and why we don't change course.

From my experience, a 360-degree feedback exercise is a good way to become better acquainted with our shadow side. It can make us more aware of our shortcomings and provide a snapshot of the gap between our imagined behavior and our real behavior. A 360-degree feedback intervention can help us see what others see. It can be a highly effective way to identify the areas we need to work on.

A 360-degree feedback process can help us reflect on what makes our behavior so inconsistent. It can highlight the discrepancies between our perceptions of what we are doing and the perceptions of others. It can motivate us to solve the puzzle of why we are subject to problem behaviors. To sum up, it may start a process of questioning why we do what we do.

By recognizing the gap between our imagined behavior and our real behavior, we can begin to truly do what we claim we've been doing but haven't.

By recognizing the gap, we can begin to truly do what we claim we've been doing but haven't. Accepting the existence of this gap allows us to reflect on what's preventing us from following through on our intentions. We may then ask ourselves why the elephant inside us is behaving this way. Why has it taken charge? And, given the force of the elephant, how much freedom of choice do we really have? This reflection may lead us to explore the pros and cons of continuing our current behavior. We might develop extreme scenarios or create a balance sheet listing the benefits and costs of continuing versus stopping such behavior. Creating awareness of these variables can be a starting point for changing inconsistent behavior.

This contemplation process may prepare us to take action, so we do things differently in the future. It can help us develop an early warning system to subvert the power of our unconscious fallback position. However, change will take a lot of practice. It will take time to internalize new ways of doing things, and it is all too easy to relapse into old habits.

ASKING FOR HELP

To deal with these intrapsychic blockages and regain a sense of control over our lives, we may need the help of an executive coach or psychotherapist. Such a person can affirm our ability to change and help us become more aware of the consequences of our problematic behavior. They can assist us in exploring the discrepancy between our problem behaviors and our goals. Furthermore, if we make serious efforts to close the gap between our intentions and our actions, these helping professionals can acknowledge our baby steps in the right direction. They can help us practice coping strategies to avoid returning to our problem behaviors. This includes processing relapses and developing plans to prevent them from happening. In sum, these professionals can help us monitor and review our progress toward long-term goals, while always reminding us that *we* are responsible for making the necessary changes.

Let's never forget that if we want to see positive changes, we must take things into our own hands. Good intentions alone are never enough.

Let's never forget that if we want to see positive changes, we must take things into our own hands. Good intentions alone are never enough. After all, people are judged by their actions. The elephant inside must stay on its best behavior for any changes to be sustainable.

In summary, we should remember that we are responsible for managing the elephant inside. This implies that we need to ride the elephant judiciously and override some of its automatic processes. As the Cretan writer Nikos Kazantzakis said, "Since we cannot change reality, let us change the eyes which see reality."[7]

There will always be times when we aren't sure why we do what we do. After all, our intrapsychic world is quite complex. Hence, we should accept that we aren't always in control. When the time comes for growth and change, we must have the courage and faith to let go. It is also fair to say that there will be many times when we will be at a loss. But if that's the case, it's a reminder that we aren't the rational actors that we imagine ourselves to be. However difficult it is to lack control, we'd better accept what's happening to us as the kind of loss that's part of the human condition.

When the time comes for growth and change, we must have the courage and faith to let go. However difficult it is to lack control, we'd better accept what's happening to us as the kind of loss that's part of the human condition.

NOTES

1   Samuel Johnson. In George Birkbeck Hill (1887). *Boswell's Life of Johnson*. Oxford: Clarendon Press, Volume 2. Journal entry from 14 April 1775.

2   Sigmund Freud (1913/1899). *The Interpretation of Dreams*. Trans. A. A. Brill. New York: The Macmillan Company.

3   John A. Bargh and Ezequiel Morsella (2008). The unconscious mind. *Perspectives on Psychological Science*, 3(1), 73–79; Emma Young (2018). Lifting the lid on the unconscious. *New Scientist*, July 25.

4   Timothy D. Wilson (2004). *Strangers to Ourselves: Discovering the Adaptive Unconscious*. Cambridge, MA: Belknap Press, an imprint of Harvard University Press.

5   Sigmund Freud (1932). *New Introductory Lectures on Psychoanalysis and Other Works*. The Standard Edition of the Complete Psychological Works of Sigmund Freud, Volume XXII (1932–1936). London: Hogarth Press.

6   Wilson. *Strangers to Ourselves*.

7   Nikos Kazantzakis (1973/1965). The son. In *Report to Greco*. Trans. P. A. Bien. London: Faber and Faber.

2

PEOPLE DON'T QUIT JOBS; THEY QUIT BOSSES

All changes, even the most longed for, have their melancholy; for what we leave behind us is a part of ourselves: we must die to one life before we can enter another!

—Anatole France[1]

Toxic people are like a piece of gum stuck to your shoe. They're sticky and annoying, and they refuse to let you go.

—Anon.

As I said before, loss can take many different forms. People who work in organizations are no strangers to loss. Take the tale of Naomi. Lately, she's been having a hard time sleeping, troubled by recurrent nightmares. In her dreams, she finds herself in a dark parking lot with no exit. While searching for a way out, she hears footsteps approaching, causing her to panic and hide behind one of the parked cars. Suddenly, a dark figure with a faintly familiar face approaches her. She tries to run away, but her feet feel like lead, leaving her immobilized and filled with terror. Then, drenched in sweat, she wakes up.

Reluctantly, but encouraged by her husband, Naomi decided to see a coach. To her surprise, the discussions with him turned out to be quite constructive. Through free association exercises, he helped her realize that the dark figure she dreaded in these nightmares reminded her of her boss. She admitted that she often felt anxious about going to work.

Most of the emotions triggered at work were linked to her boss's demands and attitude towards her. Naomi began to recognize the link between her

DOI: 10.4324/9781003651260-4

boss and her anxious thoughts, restless nights, and recurring nightmares. She also started to see that her negative state of mind was stifling her creativity, motivation, and productivity. Ironically, as her coach pointed out, while her boss was pushing for greater performance, he undermined her confidence and diminished her abilities.

Working for bad bosses is one of the major stressors in a
person's working life.

Sadly, workplace stress due to bad bosses is more common than most people realize. When bosses behave inappropriately, have unrealistic expectations, or aren't supportive of work–life issues, it's no surprise that health suffers. In fact, working for bad bosses is one of the major stressors in a person's working life. It has been linked to high levels of anxiety, depression, insomnia, high blood pressure, and even premature aging. If these stress reactions aren't worrisome enough, working for a bad boss has also been associated with unhealthy behavior patterns such as smoking, excessive alcohol use, drug abuse, and overeating.[2] In addition, when people experience high levels of work stress, tensions can spill over to their partner, spouse, or children, impacting family well-being.

There exists a broad spectrum of bad bosses, from micromanagers to narcissists to bullies. Bad bosses also include those with extreme mood swings and outlandish expectations, as well as those who hoard information, avoid conflict, never give positive feedback, or are never available. These various characteristics make these difficult people to work for. Bosses who combine psychopathic and narcissistic (the "dark dyad") traits can have an extremely toxic influence. In addition, these individuals are often quite Machiavellian. They tend to take advantage of their subordinates, take credit for their work, are overly critical, and generally behave inappropriately. Overall, these people create a highly dysfunctional work environment.[3]

Bosses who combine psychopathic and narcissistic (the
"dark dyad") traits can have an extremely toxic influence.

Aside from being a nightmare for their subordinates, bad bosses can have a very negative effect on the general work climate. Their demands and behaviors sap people of their willpower and motivation, contribute to mental fatigue, and impair performance. When such bosses play their subordinates against each other, what should be a culture of positive competitiveness can turn into a culture of mistrust, backstabbing, and upheaval. This environment can lead to increased absenteeism due to mental health issues and higher staff turnover as employees quit to escape their toxic boss.

That said, letting go of a job can be quite difficult; it isn't easy, and it may require a lot of courage. It is a form of loss that can take a long time to work through, bringing up many feelings. However, whatever we plan to do, we also need to consider the cost of hanging on. If we persevere, are we prepared to pay the price? How will staying in the job affect our mental health? Considering this, have we weighed the costs and benefits of letting go? Clearly, the choices we make will greatly determine the kind of future we want.

When bad bosses play their subordinates against each other, what should be a culture of positive competitiveness can turn into a culture of mistrust, backstabbing, and upheaval.

HOW TO DEAL WITH TOXIC BOSSES

If, like Naomi, you have a manager who calls you at all hours and expects you to cancel your vacation plans for meetings, it's time to reset expectations with the boss or HR or change jobs. Based on my experience, here are several options you can pursue when dealing with toxic bosses.

- *Establish boundaries.* One of the first and most important things to do is to set boundaries and explain what you're prepared and not prepared to do. Boundary setting involves the subtle art of saying "no" to unrealistic expectations. One approach is to explain your current workload to your boss and have a serious discussion about realistic benchmarks and time-frames. While holding this discussion, you could also take the opportunity to explore the pressures your boss is under. Understanding why your boss behaves the way he or she does can be helpful. A better sense of his or her situation may help align expectations and arrive at win–win solutions. This could be a game-changer.
- *Provide upward feedback on leadership style.* If setting boundaries does not work and you still feel extremely pressured, it may be time to address the elephant in the room: how your boss's leadership style is affecting you. This conversation can be delicate. When you challenge a bad boss, you may also challenge the people who put them in that position, and they may not be prepared to address the dysfunctional behavior. Therefore, you may want HR to be part of the conversation. To enlist HR's support, build a case on how your boss's behavior affects not only your mental health but also that of others in the organization. Focus on the impact on overall performance.

Collect and share with HR detailed records of your boss's dysfunctional behavior. During the discussion, make them aware of the problems and offer concrete and constructive suggestions to improve the situation. Just be mindful that whistleblowers never win popularity contests.

When you challenge a bad boss, you may also challenge the people who put them in that position, and they may not be prepared to address the dysfunctional behavior.

- *Transfer out of the position.* If your boss cannot or is not willing to change, but you like working for your present company, another option is to switch departments. You could try to make a lateral move, which would require some serious networking. Start by dropping hints to other senior executives that you're looking for responsibilities that aren't available in your current role. However, avoid badmouthing or gossiping about your boss. It's not wise to go to war with them. Instead, focus on your own strengths and achievements.
- *Quit.* If your work situation continues to affect your health, self-esteem, and general well-being negatively, and if there's no way to get transferred or improve the situation, it may be time to leave your current employer. Instead of hoping that your relationship with your toxic boss will change, focus on finding a work environment where your talents are truly valued. This involves broadening your external network and gaining a new perspective on ideal career options. You may realize that competitors in your industry are looking for what you can offer. Do due diligence to ensure that you don't end up with another bad boss.
- *Get support.* Looking after your mental health is crucial for a well-lived life. Everyone needs support networks. If you feel stressed out due to a poor working relationship, it may be time to seek out a coach, mentor, or other trained helping professional who can guide you in reassessing your options. These people can steer you towards more rewarding career opportunities. They may also help you work through the loss that accompanies leaving an organization.

Returning to Naomi, she realized that, for her, the best way to move forward was to get out. Hopefully, as her coach mentioned, she would be able to look back at what had happened to her as a learning opportunity. In hindsight, maybe it sharpened her management skills and taught her how to avoid becoming a bad boss herself.

Looking after your mental health is crucial
for a well-lived life.

As we spend a considerable part of our lives at work, it needs to be a positive learning environment that doesn't compromise our mental or physical health. When people are mentally healthy, they can work at their full potential, cope with the normal stresses of life, and make positive contributions to society. At work, everyone deserves to be respected and treated well. As Naomi's case illustrates, nobody should choose a toxic job over their mental health. If that's the case, they should cut their losses—difficult as this may be—and move on. Some people think holding on makes us strong, but sometimes it is the act of letting go that does so. This letting go doesn't mean that life is over. On the contrary, it can be a new beginning, and the loss can be managed.

NOTES

1   Anatole France (1890/1881). *The Crime of Sylvestre Bonnard*. New York: Harper and Bros, Pt. II, Ch. 4.
2   Ui Young Sun, Haoying Xu, and Seokhwa Yun (2023). What does leaders' abuse mean to me? Psychological empowerment as the key mechanism explaining the relationship between abusive supervision and taking charge. *Group and Organization Management*. https://doi.org/10.1177/10596011231204387
3   Manfred F. R. Kets de Vries and Danny Miller (1991). *The Neurotic Organization: Diagnosing and Changing Counterproductive Styles of Management*. San Francisco, CA: Jossey-Bass.

3

LOSS AND RENEWAL IN RETIREMENT

The journey of a thousand miles commenced when the foot was placed on the ground.

—Lao Tzu[1]

Age imprints more wrinkles in the mind than it does on the face.

—Michel de Montaigne[2]

Men grow old because they stop playing, and not conversely.

—Stanley Hall[3]

LETTING GO

As we saw in the last chapter, letting go of a job can cause much grief. But that's not the only form of work-related loss. Retirement can also lead to heartbreak and great sorrow. Take Nicolas. He really enjoyed working in the construction industry. Thanks to much hard work, he had reached a senior position in the organization. But recently, he had become vaguely aware that the clock was ticking. The company had a mandatory retirement age, but Nicolas had never given it much thought, busy as he was. Whenever he thought about it, he figured that retirement would give him more time to perfect his golf game and travel with his wife to places they had always dreamed of seeing.

Letting go of a job can cause much grief. But that's not the only form of work-related loss—retirement can also lead to heartbreak and great sorrow.

DOI: 10.4324/9781003651260-5

When the retirement date arrived, he was delighted to see how his colleagues went out of their way to celebrate his achievements. Many great speeches were given, and it was a memorable day. The day after, he embarked with his wife on a lengthy cruise in Southeast Asia—also a fantastic experience.

Unfortunately, Nicolas's upbeat mood didn't last very long. While the idea of golf was very attractive when he didn't have the time to play, it was quite different playing golf day after day. It didn't provide the same satisfaction as making interesting deals in the office. Deep down, he missed being at work. Without his job, he felt at a loss.

After his return home, Nicolas regularly caught up with his former colleagues. However, as time passed, such meetups and discussions began to peter out. Soon, he felt as though he had been forgotten by the people he once worked closely with. Sitting at home, watching the news, reading the newspapers, or playing the occasional game of golf provided him with limited stimulation. In fact, life had become tedious. He had imagined spending more time with his wife, but she was very busy with her own activities. At times, he even wondered whether his neediness was getting on her nerves. All in all, Nicolas felt quite lonely.

Nicolas became more and more morose, in a way that was noticeable to others. He began to feel resentful that the world was passing him by. Then one day, to everybody's dismay, Nicolas was found dead in his house. He had killed himself.

What happened to Nicolas? What made him decide to take his own life? Could his suicide have been prevented? Was his suicide related to the fact that he never seriously thought about what came after retirement? Was it because he had never deeply addressed what retirement would mean to him? Could he have taken various measures to prevent this fatal decision?

For many people, retirement can be a great blessing. After years of hard work, the world is now their oyster. Such people have often acquired sufficient resources to give them numerous options. Had Nicolas properly planned the rest of his life before his retirement, he might have discovered countless, meaningful possibilities for spending his time and energy. Unfortunately, caught up in day-to-day routines at work, he had never given the matter much thought.

As Nicolas's example shows, retirement comes with various life changes. Before, his work routines had provided structure and meaning to his life. But without them—and in the absence of satisfying new ones—Nicolas felt increasingly lost. Most of Nicolas's social interactions had taken place at work. Without these relationships, he felt quite isolated.

> As we now live much longer than in the past, retiring completely when we are still physically and mentally fit is not a great proposition.

While this was not the case for Nicolas, other adjustments often associated with retirement include a loss of income, contributing to financial worries. Furthermore, a decline in physical health due to aging can lead to general feelings of anxiety. Aging also sometimes aggravates lingering concerns about death.[4]

It should not come as a surprise that, for some people, retirement impacts their mental and physical health. Various studies have shown that early retirement can cause a decline in memory and brain functions.[5] Consequently, as we now live much longer than in the past, retiring completely when we are still physically and mentally fit is not a great proposition.

If Nicolas had taken the time to consider the implications of retirement carefully, he could have put in place a more phased process. Instead of being shocked by the sudden transition, he could have disengaged gradually. For example, he could have explored his passions, skills, and interests, and tried new activities. He could have created for himself a mix of part-time jobs, freelance work, or consulting assignments to continue using his many talents. Given his financial security, he could have maintained a great work–life balance. Instead, Nicolas only focused on improving his golf game, which gave him very little satisfaction.

> For people in good mental and physical health, retirement does not have to be synonymous with loss or a retreat from life; it doesn't mean they have to feel lost. Instead, it could be a chance to explore new interests and identities.

For people in good mental and physical health, retirement does not have to be synonymous with loss or a retreat from life; it doesn't mean they have to feel lost. Instead, it could be a chance to explore new interests and identities. In fact, as we live longer, there is no reason to stick to one career. People can adopt a portfolio career approach, assuming a variety of roles rather than one job at a single organization. The advantages of a portfolio career include greater work–life balance, flexibility, variety, multiple income streams, and the ability to pursue individual interests. With this in mind, what are some options for "what's next"?

- *Be more present.* One of the most enriching options is to be more present with family and friends. At this point in life especially, retirement allows us to strengthen relationships with loved ones and create cherished memories with children, grandchildren, and other family members.
- *Pursue hobbies.* A popular option is to pursue hobbies and dedicate ourselves to activities that we didn't have time for during our working years. Whether it's painting, gardening, cooking, writing, playing a musical instrument, or traveling, we can now devote ourselves to the things we always loved and that will keep us mentally active. Importantly, physical fitness is essential for maintaining a healthy and vital lifestyle. For example, we could consider joining fitness classes, going for long walks, swimming, or participating in other sports or exercises.
- *Travel.* Another popular option is to travel. Retirement opens up opportunities to explore the world and have new experiences. We now have the time to visit places we always wanted to see, encounter different cultures, create special moments, and build new memories.
- *Give back.* Many retirees find great fulfillment in giving back to their communities by volunteering for charitable organizations, schools, universities, hospitals, or other causes they care about. For example, we can serve as mentors, coaches, or teachers to the younger generation. In addition, we can support causes we believe in by donating time, money, or other resources to make a positive impact. It is the best time to "make our mark" on the world through caring for others.
- *Lifelong learning.* Another opportunity after retirement is to pursue new educational avenues. Lifelong learning can be incredibly enriching. Universities, colleges, and online learning platforms now offer classes or workshops on many subjects. It could even be the beginning of a part-time teaching career. Other learning paths include pursuing spiritual and emotional growth through meditation, yoga, or attending spiritual gatherings.
- *Other ways of working.* If we enjoy working and would like to continue, we can engage in part-time or freelance opportunities. We can perhaps assume the role of non-executive director at companies interested in our expertise. Others might explore entrepreneurship by starting a small business they've always dreamed of.
- *Join clubs and organizations.* Another option is to join clubs or associations. Whether it's a book club, a hiking group, or a community organization, joining social clubs can lead to new friendships based on shared interests.

A critical factor for mental health is to devote energy to building and maintaining strong social relationships.

For Nicolas, the key to deciding his next steps would have been to reflect on what would have brought him joy, satisfaction, and fulfillment. What energized him? Knowing that his retirement was approaching, he should have prepared for this transition. Recognizing the upcoming cutoff date, he could have crafted a disengagement plan aligned with his values, interests, and desires—and those of his significant other. He should have explored his inner world to identify the activities that would bring meaning to his life. Simultaneously, he should have devoted energy to building and maintaining strong social relationships—a critical factor for mental health. Before retiring, he should have laid the groundwork to enjoy the fruits of his labor while continuing to lead a purposeful and rewarding life.[6] Had he done so, he might not have felt such a sense of loss, and a tragedy might have been avoided.

NOTES

1   Lao Tzu (1905/6th century BC). Chapter LXIV. In *The Tao Teh King: A Short Study in Comparative Religion*. Trans. C. Spurgeon Medhurst. Chicago, IL: Theosophical Book Concern.

2   Michel de Montaigne (1877/1580). *Essays of Michel de Montaigne*. Trans. Charles Cotton. Ed. William Carew Hazlitt. London: Reeves and Turner, Vol. III, Book III, Chapter II.

3   Stanley Hall (1904). *Adolescence: Its Psychology and Its Relations to Physiology, Anthropology, Sociology, Sex, Crime, Religion and Education*. New York: D. Appleton and Company, Volume 1, Chapter 3, p. 235.

4   Manfred F. R. Kets de Vries (2014). Death and the executive: Encounters with the "stealth" motivator. *Organizational Dynamics*, 43(4), 247–328.

5   Plamen Nikolov and Alan Adelman (2020). Pension policies, retirement and human capital depreciation in late adulthood. IZA DP No. 13932. IZA Institute of Labor Economics, Bonn; Plamen Nikolov and Md Shahadath Hossain (2022). Do pension benefits accelerate cognitive decline? Evidence from rural China. IZA DP No. 15742. IZA Institute of Labor Economics, Bonn; Jo Mhairi Hale, Maarten J. Bijlsma, and Angelo Lorenti (2021). Does postponing retirement affect cognitive function? A counterfactual experiment to disentangle life course risk factors. *SSM Population Health*, September 15; Baowen Xue, Dorina Cadar, Maria Fleischmann, Stephen Stansfeld, Ewan Carr, Mika Kivimäki, Anne McMunn, and Jenny Head (2018). Effect of retirement on cognitive function: The Whitehall II cohort study. *European Journal of Epidemiology*, 33(10), 989–1001.

6   Manfred F. R. Kets de Vries (2021). *Quo Vadis? The Existential Challenges of Leaders*. London: Palgrave Macmillan.

4

IS AI THE BOGEYMAN OF OUR AGE?

We are all in the gutter, but some of us are looking at the stars.

—Oscar Wilde[1]

The greatest pleasure in life is doing what people say you cannot do.

—Walter Bagehot[2]

Let's now focus on another kind of loss: the feeling of loss due to artificial intelligence (AI). You might ask, what kind of loss am I referring to? It's a surprising one. When I give lectures on leadership and related topics, recently the topic of AI almost always comes up during the question-and-answer period. From the questions I receive, it's clear that many people find AI to be a very worrisome development. There's a palpable sense among these individuals that the world as they know it is fast disappearing.

Many people find it quite scary to see how AI is rapidly revolutionizing industries, influencing productivity, and shaping the future of technology around the world. Others, however, seem almost oblivious to what's happening—likely a state of denial. They refuse to acknowledge that AI has become so ubiquitous that one hardly notices its presence. Regardless of their reactions, most people are confused about what the rise of AI will mean for them. They have lost their footing.

It's clear that many people find AI to be a very worrisome development. There's a palpable sense among these individuals that the world as they know it is fast disappearing.

DOI: 10.4324/9781003651260-6

The nature of the questions I hear makes it sound like AI is a "black box" where mysterious things happen. The mystery quickly transforms into fear and distrust. Admittedly, some concerns are valid. Let's dive in.

One of the most significant fears is job displacement. As machines perform tasks at lower costs and greater efficiency than humans, AI will eliminate certain job categories. The impact of AI could accelerate income inequalities and even create poverty for some.

Other concerns about AI are more ethical in nature. Generally, these fears revolve around the loss of control and unease about AI's impact on human relationships. Many people worry that AI will invade privacy and cause social harm. They fear that the abundance of deepfake data could make it difficult to discern what is real. These concerns include the potential use of AI for malicious purposes such as misinformation campaigns, cyberattacks, and the development of autonomous weapons. Indeed, many autocratic regimes, such as Russia and North Korea, have been exploiting the darker capabilities of AI.

Human beings have a rich fantasy life, and
their worries often take on an existential nature.

Beyond these realistic concerns, we shouldn't underestimate the more imaginary ones. Human beings have a rich fantasy life, and their worries often take on an existential nature. Some fear that AI systems will become so advanced that they will turn into conscious organisms, surpassing human intelligence. And as these systems keep self-learning, there's a fear that they will become uncontrollable, leading to unforeseen, catastrophic side effects. Some even imagine that AI could cause the mass destruction of life on Earth.

AI occupies a strange position, having a decades-
long history while still feeling wholly futuristic.

What these individuals don't seem to realize is that AI occupies a strange position, having a decades-long history while still feeling wholly futuristic. AI doomsayers should remember that this isn't the first time we've faced industry disruptions—from automation in manufacturing to e-commerce in retail. Tales of sentient and potentially malevolent technologies date back not just decades but millennia. The fears around AI echo past reactions to earlier innovations. In fact, every significant progress achieved by humanity has been met with skepticism.

Every significant progress achieved by
humanity has been met with skepticism.

A good illustration of these concerns is the reaction, in the late eighteenth century, of British weavers and textile workers who objected to the introduction of mechanized looms and knitting frames. To protect their jobs, they formed groups called Luddites that attempted to destroy these new machines. But they weren't the only ones fearing they would lose out. *Neophobia*, the irrational fear or dislike of anything new or unfamiliar, has always characterized humans. For example, at the dawn of electrification, some exaggerated the dangers of electricity, spreading frightening stories of people who had died of electrocution. Similarly, when television was introduced, there were fears about its potential to increase violence due to the popularity of violent programming. In the 1960s, apprehension arose about the impact of robotics, with many fearing that this cutting-edge technology would supplant human labor. Continuing this saga of resistance to change, the widespread introduction of personal computers in the 1980s and 1990s also sparked fears of job loss.

Neophobia, the irrational fear or dislike of anything
new or unfamiliar, has always characterized humans.

In hindsight, although many of these technological breakthroughs brought dislocation and hardships, it is clear that they also came with great advantages. In most instances, they stimulated the creation of other, perhaps even better, jobs.

Humans tend to fear what they don't understand. They become apprehensive when they are at a loss. The current AI-phobia is creating paranoid fears that people will lose out in a world devaluing human creativity and ingenuity. The fear that AI will replace humans has been propagated by many science fiction writers. They were the ones who introduced the idea that a conscious, super-intelligent AI could, either through malevolence or by accident, kill us all. Such stories threaten our deep-seated need for control and safety. The fear that AI could run amok has been exacerbated by numerous films, TV shows, comic books, and other popular media featuring robots or computers subjugating or exterminating the human race. Stanley Kubrick's movie *2001: A Space Odyssey*, with the HAL computer taking control, or films like *The Terminator* or *The Matrix* are prime examples.

Put succinctly, AI has become the new bogeyman—a symbolic representation of people's fear of the unknown. This menacing and elusive apparition lurks in the darkest corners of our imagination, creating a great sense of unease. Like the bogeyman in horror movies, AI is a metaphor for real-life terrors, both captivating and terrifying many people.

> AI has become the new bogeyman—a symbolic representation of people's fear of the unknown.

The basic utility of the bogeyman has always been to instill fear in children, making them more likely to comply with parental authority and societal rules. In that respect, the bogeyman represents the fears and anxieties that children face as they navigate the complexities of the world. In fact, his presence seems to be a natural part of the cognitive and emotional development of every human being. From an evolutionary perspective, this mysterious menace also connects with the experiences of our Paleolithic ancestors, who were exposed to the vagaries of their environment. In their unpredictable world, bogeymen were everywhere—in the form of thunder, lightning, floods, predatory animals, and other calamities.

Considering *Homo sapiens'* developmental history, these childish fears about bogeymen have not disappeared. Consciously or unconsciously, these fears persist in adulthood. They symbolize the anxieties that linger just beneath the surface, tapping into primal fears. The bogeyman's endurance throughout history demonstrates the universal fascination with the darker side of human nature. However, given our understanding of human nature, we must face the irrational fears of loss associated with AI. We shouldn't forget that faith in technology has been a cornerstone of modern society. As just mentioned, we've all been using various forms of AI for a long time, often without realizing it. And the bogeyman hasn't yet come to get us. The fear that AI will overthrow humanity is grounded in misconceptions about what AI actually is.

> The bogeyman's endurance throughout history demonstrates the universal fascination with the darker side of human nature.

At its core, AI is simply a field of computer science focused on creating intelligent systems capable of performing tasks that require human collaboration. AI is just another tool for improving human productivity, like previous technological advances such as the stone axe, the telephone, the personal computer, the Internet, or the smartphone.

If we really think about it, the most serious loss we face is not from AI acting against humanity but from the willful misuse of AI by other human beings. It is, in reality, *Homo sapiens* who behaves exactly as we fear AI would. It is *Homo sapiens* who has become unpredictably uncontrollable. It is *Homo sapiens* who acts in ways that bring about inequality and injustice. And it is *Homo sapiens* who is capable of the mass destruction of life on Earth. Keeping these facts in mind, we would be wise to remember that it is possible to develop AI responsibly and ethically. To achieve this, however, we must manage the irrational fears associated with the bogeyman. If we do so, we may realize that our feelings of loss are very much self-inflicted.

> If we really think about it, the most serious loss we face is not from AI acting against humanity but from the willful misuse of AI by other human beings.

NOTES

1 Oscar Wilde (1893). *Lady Windermere's Fan*. London: Samuel French.
2 Walter Bagehot (1915/1853). *The Works and Life of Walter Bagehot*. Ed. Mrs. Russell Barrington. London: Longmans, Green, and Co., Vol. 1, Shakespeare essay.

5

A KING'S TALE

Is life not a hundred times too short for us—to bore ourselves?

—Friedrich Nietzsche[1]

The history of the world has been one not of conquest, as supposed; it has been one of ennui.

—Helen Westley[2]

Loss has many facets, as we've seen so far. Yet another aspect of loss is exemplified by the following tale of a king. Though presented as a fairytale, this story symbolically reflects the experiences I've observed in many executives. It highlights the loss of interest in life—the destructive power of boredom.

Once upon a time, in a faraway land, there lived a king who, after many heroic deeds, fell into a deep state of boredom. He grew tired of presiding over banquets, waving from the royal balcony, and cutting ribbons at ceremonies. Even attending jousts and events held in his honor became a burden. The courtiers, noticing his plight, tried everything to amuse him. They feared his boredom would spiral out of control, for a bored king is capable of anything—especially the worst.

They presented exotic animals, prepared mouthwatering dishes, and paraded beautiful women before him, but nothing sparked his interest. The king's boredom had grown so intense that he seemed to have lost even the desire to desire. His grumpiness worried the courtiers further, as they sensed his boredom might turn into disillusionment, self-pity, and ultimately chaos. Desperate, they sought a solution.

DOI: 10.4324/9781003651260-7

The grand vizier issued a proclamation: whoever could relieve the king's boredom would be richly rewarded. People from across the land—poets, jugglers, philosophers, and more—came to amuse him, but nothing worked. As the king grew more morose, his selfishness increased, making life miserable for his entourage.

The antidote to boredom lies in purpose, empathy, compassion, and gratitude.

Finally, the court jester made a dramatic entry, saying, "Your Majesty, we've searched far and wide for a cure to your boredom. In the royal library, I found an ancient book of magic. It advises that you issue a proclamation granting all your subjects two weeks of paid leave and gifting every child with toys. In addition, to celebrate your upcoming birthday, there should be a grand party with food, music, and dancing. This would allow Your Majesty to express gratitude to your faithful subjects."

The king called the jester an idiot for suggesting such extravagance and ordered his execution. But before the knights could carry out the order, the jester continued, "This book also praises you as the greatest king who ever lived, whose subjects respect and admire you. It further advises that no one in the kingdom should go hungry and that joy should spread throughout the land. The book reveals that the antidote to boredom lies in purpose, empathy, compassion, and gratitude."

Intrigued, the king relented. Something within him stirred, and to the court's amazement, he decided to follow the jester's advice and declare a day of celebration for his subjects. For the first time in a long while, appreciating the gratitude expressed by his subjects, the king smiled. And this time, the smile lasted. Then he cried out, "Squires, bring me my hunting clothes! Before I devote myself to creating a better life for my people, I too shall celebrate."

The king had learned several important lessons. He realized that to prevent boredom, he needed dreams bigger than himself, dreams that included others.

The king had learned several important lessons. He realized that to prevent boredom, he needed dreams bigger than himself, dreams that included others. He discovered that selfless acts could bring meaning to his life, that showing compassion and empathy could build deeper connections, and that gratitude could be a powerful cure for boredom.

The king saw that he had failed to pay attention to his inner world and that life wasn't about superficial pleasures. By focusing on others rather than himself, he could find the joy that had eluded him for so long. Giving was better than receiving. And if he devoted himself wholeheartedly to meaningful activities, he could find meaning. As Blaise Pascal once observed, "Man finds nothing so intolerable as to be in a state of complete rest, without passions, without occupation, without diversion, without effort."[3]

We may even need to pity those who
have everything handed to them.

In fact, the story suggests that we may even need to pity those who have everything handed to them. Boredom, despite an abundance of distractions, can be a common cause of unhappiness among the very wealthy, whereas those who face challenges are less easily bored.

A life without challenge can lead to feelings of loss.

The king's tale also illustrates that a life without challenge can lead to feelings of loss. When life becomes too comfortable, it can breed boredom, where even simple pleasures, like satisfying hunger or the passions of love, lose their appeal. To avoid boredom, we must recognize that a certain level of anxiety and tension is necessary. When we possess everything and have nothing left to aspire to, we risk losing the will to live.

When people can obtain a prize without effort, the prize holds little value. For instance, why play cards if you know you can't lose? And if the player is a king, his courtiers will often make sure he always wins so that he doesn't get angry. But what thrill is there in playing cards without any risk? None at all.

To avoid boredom, we must recognize that a certain level of
anxiety and tension is necessary. When we possess everything
and have nothing left to aspire to, we risk losing the will to live.

People like this king are often flattered, pampered, and waited on too much. But boredom becomes inevitable in a life dedicated solely to pleasure. A king's courtiers will often anticipate his needs before he even thinks of them. However, these efforts may backfire, and kings may find themselves profoundly bored, at a loss as to how to live their lives.

Boredom becomes inevitable in a life dedicated solely to pleasure.

For the king in our story, it was crucial he regained his sense of wonder, re-engaged with his passions, and reconnected with what truly mattered to him. To be whole again, he needed to escape the black hole of depressive thoughts. Ultimately, the king had to realize that life is never boring—boredom is a choice.

Life is never boring—boredom is a choice.

NOTES

1 Friedrich Nietzsche (1923/1886). *Beyond Good and Evil*. Trans. Helen Zimmern. London: George Allen & Unwin, Aphorism 227.
2 Helen Westley. Quoted in Djuna Barnes (1917). The confessions of Helen Westley. *New York Morning Telegraph Sunday Magazine*, 23 September.
3 Blaise Pascal (2011/1670). *Pensées*. CreateSpace Independent Publishing Platform.

6

IN PRAISE OF BOREDOM

Soon he felt rising in his soul a desire for desires—boredom.

—Leo Tolstoy[1]

She refused to be bored chiefly because she wasn't boring. She was conscious that the things she did were the things she had always wanted to do.

—Zelda Fitzgerald[2]

The tale of the king in the previous chapter vividly demonstrates the destructive power of boredom, revealing how it can erode even the most privileged lives, leading to a profound sense of loss and disconnection. As we've seen, the antidote to this debilitating state lies not in the accumulation of more possessions or fleeting pleasures but in cultivating a life of purpose, empathy, compassion, and gratitude.

> Boredom can erode even the most privileged lives,
> leading to a profound sense of loss and disconnection.

Boredom, however, isn't exclusive to the very wealthy, such as those able to purchase extravagant villas, impressive yachts, private airplanes, renowned art collections, or great vineyards. While historically associated with the social elite—the leisure class—boredom affects people across all social strata, even if the causes differ. Boredom is an existential vacuum that we all encounter at some point in our lives. It's a universal experience that spans all ages. There's

DOI: 10.4324/9781003651260-8

also a socio-cultural dimension: as civilization advances, opportunities for boredom increase, leaving us unsure how to navigate life's vicissitudes.

> Boredom is an existential vacuum that we
> all encounter at some point in our lives.

Our ancestors were primarily focused on survival, spending most of their time securing food and shelter. They had little time to be bored, given the dangers they faced. Even a few hundred years ago, essential tasks that we now take for granted required significant time and effort. Today, however, our minds must work harder to find activities that occupy the same amount of time. Moreover, advances in technology and the fast pace of modern life have shortened our attention span. Addicted to a constant stream of stimuli, we are more susceptible to boredom.

> As civilization advances, opportunities for boredom increase,
> leaving us unsure how to navigate life's vicissitudes.

Philosophical reflections on boredom date back to Roman times, with the philosopher Seneca lamenting the monotony of life. He wrote, "Surely I will yawn, I will sleep, I will eat, I will be thirsty, I will be cold, I will be hot. Is there no end?"[3]

Centuries later, medieval monks struggled with "acedia," a state of listlessness or spiritual apathy, particularly during the hours of ten to two—the "noonday demon"—when the repetitiveness of their lives led them to exhaustion and restlessness. The Church saw acedia as a dangerous form of spiritual alienation, a rejection of the world and its creator, resulting in troubling feelings of loss.

The English word "boredom" was coined in the early nineteenth century and entered public consciousness through Charles Dickens's novel *Bleak House*. But he wasn't the only one interested in this subject. Anton Chekhov frequently explored boredom in his works, as did Leo Tolstoy, who described it as a "desire for desires."[4]

> Medieval monks struggled with "acedia," a state of
> listlessness or spiritual apathy, particularly during the hours of
> ten to two—the "noonday demon"—when the repetitiveness
> of their lives led them to exhaustion and restlessness.

Philosophers have also grappled with the concept. The German thinker Arthur Schopenhauer viewed boredom as one of the "two enemies of human happiness," the other one being pain.[5] He also claimed that if life were devoid of all difficulty, "men would either die of boredom or hang themselves."[6]

Denmark's philosopher Søren Kierkegaard wrote:

> Since boredom advances and boredom is the root of all evil, no wonder, then, that the world goes backwards, that evil spreads. This can be traced back to the very beginning of the world. The gods were bored; therefore, they created human beings.[7]

Friedrich Nietzsche, another German thinker, later echoed the sentiment: "Against boredom even gods struggle in vain."[8]

Boredom is often linked with alienation, anomie, disenchantment, and depression—conditions that reflect our humanity and make feelings of loss an inevitable part of life.

The British philosopher Bertrand Russell suggested that "boredom is therefore a vital problem for the moralist, since at least half the sins of mankind are caused by the fear of it."[9] Always ready to give his two cents, the Frenchman Jean-Paul Sartre viewed boredom as a form of nausea and as an estrangement from the world.[10]

Boredom is often linked with alienation, anomie, disenchantment, and depression—conditions that reflect our humanity and make feelings of loss an inevitable part of life. It leads to an uncomfortable state of wanting to do something but also not wanting to do anything—a tense space between action and inaction. Boredom occurs when we may feel energetic but have nowhere to direct our energy. We become impassive, fatigued, and restless. We feel lost.

Boredom leads to an uncomfortable state of wanting to do something but also not wanting to do anything—a tense space between action and inaction.

This combination of lethargy and restlessness distinguishes boredom from apathy. Boredom stems from recognizing that our current situation is no longer stimulating, leading to a desire for change. In contrast, apathy is characterized by a lack of motivation and an absence of any desire to seek alternatives.

EVOLUTIONARY ADVANTAGES

From an evolutionary perspective, boredom can be seen as a survival mechanism. *Homo sapiens* has always been driven by two primary goals—survival and reproduction. When socio-cultural factors overshadow these goals, boredom may arise as an evolutionary warning signal, urging us to refocus on essential activities.

This evolutionary lens suggests that boredom may have played a crucial role in our progress as a species. The sheer frequency with which boredom is experienced across cultures suggests its importance for human growth and development. While contentment can lead to complacency—a risky evolutionary strategy—boredom pushes humans to seek new horizons, whether by moving to new locations, trying new foods, or seeking new mates. Boredom, in essence, might have expanded the repertoire of human possibilities, creating future options beyond the "boring" present.

The sheer frequency with which boredom is experienced across cultures suggests its importance for human growth and development.

It's possible that only the most evolved species, with developed consciousness, are capable of boredom. This consciousness of repetition could prompt reflection and a realization that change is needed. Boredom may have driven our early ancestors to explore, contributing to survival and social change.

In this way, boredom may have played an important role in the rise and fall of civilizations. Even today, boredom pushes us to try new activities or explore new interests. Thus, we should be grateful for boredom as it can steer us towards realizing our potential and living fuller, more meaningful lives.

We should be grateful for boredom as it can steer us towards realizing our potential and living fuller, more meaningful lives.

THE MANY COLORS OF BOREDOM

Boredom can stem from various factors, including gender, age, education, and personality. Men, children, and adolescents, who often feel constrained by rules, are more prone to boredom. There's also a link between low educational attainment and boredom. It might be that people with less education don't have as rich an internal life compared with people who are more educated. Extroverts and those with neurodevelopmental disorders such as attention-deficit/hyperactivity disorder (ADHD) or autism spectrum disorders (ASD) often suffer from boredom.[11] After all, it's hard to stay engaged when you have difficulties concentrating.

As boredom is such a disturbing feeling, people do all kinds of things to seek relief. Sometimes they engage in self-destructive behavior. In fact, boredom is said to be a significant factor in behaviors such as drug addiction, alcoholism, compulsive gambling, and eating disorders. It can also be linked to low performance at work or in school.[12] These behaviors may be a kind of "boredom EpiPen" for those lacking the mental resources to care for themselves.

Self-destructive behaviors may be a kind of "boredom EpiPen" for those lacking the mental resources to care for themselves.

Philobats and ocnophils

Some people seem to have a greater need for external stimulation than others. We can even classify people depending on their motivational tendencies. For example, there are people who possess a "Type T" or thrill-seeking personality. They seek novel, complex, and intense experiences.[13] These individuals are addicted to stimulation and excitement, and they may self-medicate against boredom by taking extreme risks. Without this stimulation, they may become bored, depressed, and at a loss for how to live their lives.

In fact, long before the introduction of the concept of Type T personalities, Hungarian-British psychiatrist Michael Balint distinguished between two types of people: ocnophils and philobats.[14] Ocnophils are non-adventurous and driven by a fear of abandonment. They seek safety in familiar environments. Philobats, on the other hand, are more independent and thrill-seeking. They are like adrenaline junkies who thrive on danger and often land in trouble. The most timid of the ocnophils and the most intrepid of the philobats—those at both extremes—tend to be more prone to boredom.

The most timid of the ocnophils and the most intrepid of the philobats—those at both extremes—tend to be more prone to boredom.

The repetitiveness of work

Work is often seen as the obvious escape from boredom. As a proverb goes, "The best cure for boredom is hard work." But ironically, when people say that they are bored, they are often referring to their work. This follows a predictable pattern. When people start a job, they feel excited and even nervous about doing something new and challenging. But as they become more familiar with the job, boredom can come to the fore and manifest itself through mind wandering.

> To feel alive, we need at least a modicum of variety.

To feel alive, we need at least a modicum of variety. Any experience that's highly predictable and repetitive is likely to become boring. When this happens, we lose our sense of "flow," a state of being fully immersed in a challenging task with clear goals and immediate feedback, as described by the Hungarian-American psychologist Mihaly Csikszentmihalyi.[15] He went on to say that understanding boredom is critical to anyone interested in "enhancing the quality of life" because this feeling has a significant effect on well-being.[16]

EMOTIONAL MANAGEMENT

Boredom is part of our emotional repertoire. As mentioned earlier, emotions act as signaling devices, alerting us to something happening within our experience and in ourselves. They tell us when something isn't right.

> Emotions act as signaling devices, alerting us to something happening within our experience and in ourselves and telling us when something isn't right. Boredom can thus be viewed as part of our emotional repertoire.

Understanding what a specific emotion signals can help us not only comprehend our current experiences but also decide our next steps. Unfortunately, many people are emotionally illiterate. Instead of paying attention to their feelings, they somaticize them—focusing on their body's reactions rather than processing the emotions. This may be due to alexithymia, a condition where people struggle to describe or identify their feelings. These individuals often confuse bodily sensations with emotions because of an inhibited inner emotional and fantasy life.[17] Alexithymia might develop as a response to emotions generating overwhelming stress and could also be linked to genetics or brain damage. In any case, this inability to decipher feelings often contributes to existential boredom and the loss of a sense of direction.

> Many people are emotionally illiterate. Instead of paying attention to their feelings, they somaticize them—focusing on their body's reactions rather than processing the emotions.

As discussed in Chapter 1, emotions should guide us. If we lack this ability, as with alexithymia, we may not understand what brings us pleasure or enjoyment. We may struggle to articulate what we desire or want from life. Unfortunately, this means that we also lose the capacity to choose appropriate goals for ourselves. Those who lack the inner resources to deal with boredom constructively often end up relying on external stimulation. However, they don't realize that the external world will always fail to provide sufficient excitement and novelty.

> Those who lack the inner resources to deal with boredom constructively often end up relying on external stimulation. However, they don't realize that the external world will always fail to provide sufficient excitement and novelty.

Autonomy

In the context of boredom, particularly in work situations, autonomy plays a crucial role. Some people feel they have little control over their actions. They tend to react instead of taking the initiative. As a result, they feel stuck and bored. They often rely on others to pull them out of their slump, a mindset commonly found in teenagers. The teenage years are often a peak period for boredom as their day-to-day activities are largely dictated by others.

> The teenage years are often a peak period for boredom as their day-to-day activities are largely dictated by others.

Episodic vs. chronic boredom

Boredom is usually episodic, but some are prone to chronic boredom, which is detrimental to mental health. Chronic boredom increases the risk of anxiety, compulsive behavior, eating disorders, and poor performance at work or school. Frequent boredom can also be a sign of depression, especially when combined with other troubling symptoms such as decreased energy, unintentional weight loss, or sleep disturbances. This type of boredom may signal deeper issues, bordering on what could be seen as a form of imaginary suicide due to a loss of interest in life.

> Chronic boredom may signal deeper issues,
> bordering on what could be seen as a form of
> imaginary suicide due to a loss of interest in life.

IN PRAISE OF BOREDOM

Perhaps, when children complain to their parents that they are bored, the most appropriate answer is "That's great. It's up to you to figure out something fun to do." Letting kids get bored occasionally can encourage them to become more adventurous. It's better not to fix a child's boredom for them, but rather to help them find their inner resources—giving them a few pointers if they feel totally lost. But what to do when we are dealing with adults? Should we let them stew in their boredom, or should we help them see its flip side?

Clearly, boredom isn't purely negative. It's not only a warning sign but also a call to action. Boredom signals that we've settled into mental cruise control and that we're failing to engage constructively with the world. It tells us to pursue something different. In fact, boredom produces an almost irresistible desire to escape, leading to either positive or negative actions.

> Boredom signals that we've settled into mental cruise
> control and that we're failing to engage constructively
> with the world. It tells us to pursue something different.

A jolt for creativity

Boredom should be seen as a clarion call for action—a message that we aren't living up to our full potential. As the German-American psychoanalyst Erich Fromm said, "Boredom is nothing but the experience of a paralysis of our productive powers."[18] It tells us to be bold and use our boredom wisely.[19]

Like other negative emotions, such as hate, disgust, envy, anger, and sadness, boredom may have evolved to push *Homo sapiens* to seek new avenues. When we feel lost, boredom provides the physiological and psychological motivation to search for new activities. It makes us realize that something is wrong or missing from our lives. It also tells us we need to evolve. Much like hunger, thirst, and loneliness, boredom is a negative feeling—a sense of loss—that motivates us to change our behavior.

> When we feel lost, boredom provides the physiological and psychological motivation to search for new activities. It makes us realize that something is wrong or missing from our lives and tells us we need to evolve.

Boredom shouldn't be seen as an end product but as a launching pad for new activities. Our brain may need a certain period of boredom—of being stuck—to reignite creativity. Boredom acts as a catalyst, urging us to break free from the routines of everyday life. In fact, boredom often precedes periods of great creativity, providing the space for new interests to emerge. Our most creative ideas often arise after periods of boredom.

When boredom sets in, our minds begin to wander, leading to daydreaming and new explorations. These processes fuel creativity and drive us to explore new horizons. As the French moralist François de La Rochefoucauld aptly noted, "Extreme boredom provides its own antidote."[20] Boredom can be a great motivator to pursue alternative goals. This sense of loss can be turned into a gain.

> When boredom sets in, our minds begin to wander, leading to daydreaming and new explorations. These processes fuel creativity and drive us to explore new horizons.

NOTES

1   Leo Tolstoy (1909/1878). *Anna Karenina.* Trans. Constance Garnett. Philadelphia, PA: G. W. Jacobs.

2   Zelda Fitzgerald (1922). Eulogy on the flapper. *Metropolitan Magazine,* June 1922.

3   Seneca (1917/c. 65 AD). On despising death. In *Epistulae Morales ad Lucilium.* Cambridge, MA: Loeb Classical Library, Volume I, Epistle 24.26.

4   Charles Dickens (1852). *Bleak House.* For Anton Chekhov, readers can refer to *A Boring Story* (1889) or *Uncle Vanya* (1897), among others. Leo Tolstoy (1878). *Anna Karenina.*

5   Arthur Schopenhauer (1969/1818). *The World as Will and Representation.* New York: Courier Dover Publications.

6   Arthur Schopenhauer (2015/1850). *On the Suffering of the World.* New York: Simon and Schuster, p. 6.

7   Søren Kierkegaard (1992/1843). *Either/Or: A Fragment of Life.* New York: Penguin Classics.

8   Friedrich W. Nietzsche (1918/1888). *The Antichrist.* Trans. H. L. Mencken. New York: Alfred A. Knopf, section 28.

9   Bertrand Russell (1932). Boredom and excitement. In *The Conquest of Happiness.* London: George Allen & Unwin, p. 61.

10 Jean-Paul Sartre. Readers can refer to *Nausea* (1938), among others.

11 Richard Smith (1981). Boredom: A review. *Human Factors, 23*(3), 329–340; Patricia Meyer Spacks (1996). *Boredom: The Literary History of a State of Mind.* Chicago, IL: The University of Chicago Press; Peter Conrad (1997). It's boring: Notes on the meanings of boredom in everyday life. *Qualitative Sociology as*

Everyday Life, 20(4), 123–133; Michael Gardiner and Julian Jason Haladyn (eds). (2016). *Boredom Studies Reader: Frameworks and Perspectives*. London: Routledge; James Danckert and John D. Eastwood (2020). *Out of My Skull: The Psychology of Boredom*. Cambridge, MA: Harvard University Press; Mariusz Finkielsztein (2023). The significance of boredom: A literature review. *Journal of Boredom Studies*, 1, 1–33.

12 Smith, Boredom: A review; Spacks, *Boredom*; Conrad, It's boring; Gardiner and Haladyn, *Boredom Studies Reader*; Danckert and Eastwood, *Out of My Skull*; Finkielsztein, The significance of boredom.

13 Marvin Zuckerman (2007). *Sensation Seeking and Risky Behavior*. Washington, DC: American Psychological Association.

14 Michael Balint (1959). *Thrills and Regressions*. New York: International University Press.

15 Mihaly Csikszentmihalyi (1990). *Flow: The Psychology of Optimal Experience*. New York: HarperCollins.

16 Mihaly Csikszentmihalyi (2000). *Beyond Boredom and Anxiety*. San Francisco, CA: Jossey-Bass Publishers, p. 444.

17 John Case Nemiah, Hararld Freyberger, and Peter Emanuel Sifneos (1970). Alexithymia: A view of the psychosomatic process. In Oscar Hill (ed.), *Modern Trends in Psychosomatic Medicine*. Vol. 3. New York: Appleton-Century-Crofts, pp. 430–439; Joyce McDougall (1989). *Theaters of the Body: A Psychoanalytic Approach to Psychosomatic Illness*. New York: Norton.

18 Erich Fromm (2013/1955). *The Sane Society*. London: Routledge, p. 202.

19 Manfred F. R. Kets de Vries (2015). Doing nothing and nothing to do: The hidden value of empty time and boredom. *Organizational Dynamics*, 44(3), 169–175; Manoush Zomorodi (2017). *Bored and Brilliant: How Time Spent Doing Nothing Changes Everything*. London: Palgrave Macmillan.

20 L'extrême ennui sert à nous désennuyer. Author's translation. François de la Rochefoucauld (1664). Maximes adressées par La Rochefoucauld à Mme de Sablé. In *Réflexions ou sentences et maxims morales*. Kindle edition [French].

7

COPING WITH BOREDOM

There is a wide-spread belief that the art of pleasing is a valuable means of making one's fortune. But to know how to be bored is an art which gives far better results.

—Nicolas de Chamfort[1]

There is no such thing on Earth as an uninteresting subject, the only thing that can exist is an uninterested person.

—G. K. Chesterton[2]

THE CHOICE OF OVERCOMING BOREDOM

It's clear that boredom is an inevitable part of the human experience. Yet, while experiencing boredom is one thing, staying bored is another matter entirely. Staying bored is more of a choice, since boredom—reflecting a loss of interest in life—is ultimately a call to action. Although there is no miracle cure for boredom, there are many actions we can take when we feel it. How do we overcome this sense of loss?

> Experiencing boredom is one thing, staying bored is another matter entirely.

The inner journey

As with any psychological issue, the first step in overcoming boredom is understanding it. Boredom suggests a disconnect between our internal and

DOI: 10.4324/9781003651260-9

external worlds, creating imbalance. If this isn't addressed, boredom can become toxic. However, embracing boredom provides a great opportunity to explore our inner life, helping us discover what truly matters—what makes us feel alive and gives us a sense of flow. Reflection becomes our first defense against this feeling of loss. After all, we cannot fully be human without reflecting on what it means to be human. Understanding ourselves guides us toward the external stimuli we need to feel fulfilled. By closely monitoring our emotions, we can identify what truly energizes us.

> Embracing boredom provides a great opportunity to explore our inner life, helping us discover what truly matters—what makes us feel alive and gives us a sense of flow.

Unfortunately, many people lack this self-awareness. They have never undertaken a journey of self-exploration, and some may even be scared to do so. They may use boredom as a defense mechanism to avoid dealing with painful, unaddressed thoughts and emotions. For these individuals, this inner journey may seem daunting.

But it doesn't have to be. If they make the effort, boredom can push them to reflect on what they enjoy, who they are, and what they aspire to achieve. This introspection can help them understand what gives life meaning and how to overcome the sense of loss. As seen with the example of the bored king in Chapter 5, the search for meaning has always been essential to the human experience.

Of course, it can be challenging to find meaning in what feels tedious. Inner journeys are not easy. However, only relying on external stimuli to feel alive isn't the answer. Bored people should realize that if they're willing to explore why they are bored, it could turn out to be an interesting and insightful adventure.

> It can be challenging to find meaning in what feels tedious.

Overload and underload

Self-awareness also helps us recognize the cognitive and emotional demands we face daily. Boredom can arise from feeling overloaded or underloaded, but understanding what drains or energizes us is key. This awareness allows us to gauge and take on challenges we can handle.

> Boredom can arise from feeling overloaded or underloaded, but understanding what drains or energizes us is key.

Belonging and transcendence

When our internal and external worlds are out of sync, we must find new ways to invigorate our senses and enrich our inner world. Relationships play a critical role in this. Intimate relationships, in particular, can become stale without imagination, often leading to boredom or even infidelity.[3] Intimate relationships often fail not because people have stopped loving but because they have stopped imagining. However, sex alone isn't good enough—a theme that will be further explored in Chapters 10 and 11.

> Intimate relationships often fail not because people have stopped loving but because they have stopped imagining.

In the context of relationships, the effort to overcome boredom can sometimes lead to a descent into promiscuity. Some people may discover that being bored alone is difficult, but being bored together can be even worse. For some, chronic boredom may become a factor leading to adultery and, ultimately, grounds for divorce.

> Some people may discover that being bored alone is difficult, but being bored together can be even worse.

Boredom doesn't just affect couples; it can arise in relationships of all kinds. When we feel this sense of loss, we naturally seek connection. As social creatures, humans thrive on meaningful relationships, and the absence of these connections can be a major cause of boredom. While some activities are fine to do alone, others can make us feel isolated, depending on our social needs. Humans need to be part of a community, so it's important to make efforts to connect with others. For example, dining alone, watching a movie alone, or strolling through a mall by yourself can all amplify feelings of loneliness. Having a friend or family member join us in these activities can make them much more enjoyable and meaningful. Exploring new relationships, embarking on a new career path, starting a new learning journey, or taking up hobbies that involve others can also be helpful. Building or revitalizing relationships can reduce feelings of boredom and help us feel less lost.

> In relationships, we can engage in activities that transcend the self and go beyond narrow personal interests.

Furthermore, in relationships we can engage in activities that transcend the self and go beyond narrow personal interests. As British author Virginia Woolf aptly stated, "Boredom is the legitimate kingdom of the philanthropic."[4] Focusing on the less fortunate helps shift our attention from self-centeredness to community-oriented pursuits. Therefore, another effective cure for boredom is to engage in endeavors that extend beyond our narrow personal interests but are extremely enriching. Community-oriented activities, such as acts of giving, can provide the satisfaction that eludes us. In other words, humanitarian and philanthropic activities can be powerful antidotes to boredom. As the king in Chapter 5 discovered, activities that benefit others also benefit us.

> Humanitarian and philanthropic activities can be powerful antidotes to boredom.

Finding help

As mentioned earlier, depression can be seen as a co-variant of boredom. When people experience feelings of hopelessness, helplessness, sadness, irritability, withdrawal from relationships, and self-blame—when they feel lost—it may be time to seek support. It's important to address these feelings before they become worse. In such cases, turning to a psychotherapist, coach, or other helping professional can be invaluable. When it comes to depression, boredom can feel like a preview of death, or even a form of death itself, as it can cripple one's spirit. However, with professional help, individuals can overcome these limiting views and rediscover a sense of purpose and passion in life.

> When it comes to depression, boredom can feel like a preview of death, or even a form of death itself, as it can cripple one's spirit.

BOREDOM AND SOCIETY

We can also look at boredom as a social disease. While external stimuli have their limits, as illustrated by the king's example, the art of living still requires them. To avoid chronic boredom, there must be a balance between our external and internal worlds. Extremes in either direction can cause problems. For instance, a tendency to isolate oneself and withdraw from social interaction is worrisome and may indicate depression. On the other hand, focusing solely on external distractions is equally concerning, as it may suggest a lack of the internal resources needed to live a fulfilling life.

> To avoid chronic boredom, there must be a balance between our external
> and internal worlds. Extremes in either direction can cause problems.

In contemporary society, people may experience boredom more frequently than in earlier centuries. With the invention of labor-saving devices, modern man might have created an environment ripe for boredom. In the past, when survival was the primary concern, boredom was most likely rare—people were too busy seeking food and shelter to have the luxury of being bored. In this sense, boredom is a relatively modern "luxury." Today, the pace of life has accelerated, which may have diminished our ability to focus and concentrate, making us more prone to boredom.

In current times, many people seem to suffer from sensory overload. There are simply too many external distractions. Paradoxically, despite living in an overly entertained society with endless ways to amuse ourselves, boredom has become more widespread, even reaching pandemic levels in some groups. Easy access to limitless entertainment may be fueling boredom rather than alleviating it. With so much stimulation, we lose the ability to discover our true interests and passions. Conditioned by sensory overload, many of us find it increasingly difficult to embrace solitude—moments that could offer reflection and an escape from boredom. Instead, we feel lost.

> Paradoxically, despite living in an overly entertained society with endless
> ways to amuse ourselves, boredom has become more widespread.

When we look at the widespread boredom of our time, we can view the endless forms of entertainment as failed attempts at self-medication. Our obsession with external sources of entertainment—TV, movies, the Internet, and video games—has ironically created a world steeped in boredom. It may also have contributed to addictive behaviors, driven by biochemical factors (such as dopamine release from pleasurable experiences), behavioral patterns (the comfort of repetition and routines), and psychological needs (the desire for social inclusion).

Nowadays, when people find themselves alone or bored, they often reach for a device that's always close at hand. These devices have become a kind of "transitional object"—what used to be a childhood teddy bear has now transformed into an iPad, iPhone, or computer.[5] To combat boredom, we constantly refresh our feeds on social media platforms like Facebook, Instagram, and X, searching for something to engage us. We may also feel compelled to make unnecessary phone calls on FaceTime, WhatsApp, or Zoom. If these won't do, we turn on the TV, expecting to find something interesting, with endless hours of content from Netflix, Amazon Prime, HBO, YouTube, and Spotify at our fingertips. But often, seeking relief on the Internet can feel like trying to drink from a fire hose—overwhelming and unfulfilling.

> When we look at the widespread boredom of our time, we can view the endless forms of entertainment as failed attempts at self-medication.

Unfortunately, these activities have become a crutch that only reinforces our avoidance of the deep anxieties that the world around us stirs. They allow us to escape from confronting what truly matters. In today's society, we struggle to sit still with our own thoughts. We've been conditioned to crave novelty and constant stimulation, making it difficult to engage in meaningful reflection.

All these distractions act as a temporary anesthetic to the overwhelming stimuli around us, a barrier against the constant noise—a quick fix for our sense of feeling lost. Unfortunately, these temporary escapes often lead to more boredom. As our tolerance for routine and repetition decreases, we find ourselves in an endless quest for new stimulation. None of this leaves us satisfied.

> As our tolerance for routine and repetition decreases, we find ourselves in an endless quest for new stimulation. None of this leaves us satisfied.

A WORD OF CAUTION

By relying mainly on external solutions to counter boredom and overcome feelings of loss, we may lose the sense of being the authors of our own lives. To truly author our lives, we must cultivate a sense of agency, exploring internally what external factors make us feel most alive. Often, boredom signals a reluctance to embrace new learning or take risks in life. However, we are far better off when we recognize boredom as the starting point of a period of great creativity. We must be vigilant in never allowing boredom to become a chronic condition. When boredom serves as a temporary signal, it becomes a tool for living a better life. As the French writer Gustave Flaubert put it, "Isn't 'not to be bored' one of the principal goals of life?"[6]

> We must be vigilant in never allowing boredom to become a chronic condition. When boredom serves as a temporary signal, it becomes a tool for living a better life.

As we've seen, boredom is a multi-faceted, enigmatic emotion. It can evoke a deep sense of loss, as though life has no meaning. However, by cultivating self-awareness, we can begin to understand why we do what we do and learn what we are all about. This, in turn, better equips us to tackle the puzzle of boredom and helps us synchronize our internal and external worlds. As we learn to use boredom to our advantage, it becomes a profound opportunity for reflection and a catalyst for seeking new experiences. Boredom, then, aids us in connecting with others, engaging with the world, and discovering a better version of ourselves. What once felt like a frightening loss can transform into a growth experience. And the key to overcoming this sense of loss may well be curiosity.

As we learn to use boredom to our advantage, it becomes a profound opportunity for reflection and a catalyst for seeking new experiences.

NOTES

1   Nicolas de Chamfort (1902/1794). *The Cynic's Breviary: Maxims and Anecdotes from Nicolas de Chamfort.* Trans. William G. Hutchison. London: E. Matthews. [Originally published as *Maximes et Pensées.*]
2   G. K. Chesterton (1905). *Heretics.* London: The Bodley Head.
3   David E. Scharff and Jill S. Scharff (1991). *Object Relations Couple Therapy.* Lanham, MD: Jason Aronson; Richard M. Alperin (2001). Barriers to intimacy: An object relations perspective. *Psychoanalytic Psychology, 18,* 137–156; Sharron Hinchliff and Merryn Gott (2004). Intimacy, commitment, and adaptation: Sexual relationships within long-term marriages. *Journal of Social and Personal Relationships, 21,* 595–609.
4   Virginia Woolf (1977). *The Diary of Virginia Woolf 1915–1919.* Ed. Anne Olivier Bell. London: Chatto and Windus, September 20, 1918.
5   Donald W. Winnicott (1971). *Playing and Reality.* London: Routledge.
6   Gustave Flaubert (1983/1850). Flaubert to his Mother—between Minia and Assiut, 23 February 1850. In *Flaubert in Egypt. A Sensibility on Tour: A Narrative Drawn from Gustave Flaubert's Travel Notes & Letters.* Trans. and ed. Francis Steegmuller. London: Michael Haag.

8

ONE IS THE LONELIEST NUMBER

Solitude, though silent as light, is, like light, the mightiest of agencies; for solitude is essential to man. All men come into this world alone; all leave it alone.
—Thomas De Quincey[1]

The greatest thing in the world is to know how to belong to oneself.
—Michel de Montaigne[2]

LONESOME AND BLUE

We've explored how boredom—a loss of interest in life—is one form of loss. Loneliness, another, highlights the challenge of forging meaningful human connections. The following story illustrates the weight of this interpersonal loss.

Nadine, a senior executive in the fashion industry, was troubled by her lack of a social life. Despite her seemingly glamorous lifestyle and many business contacts, she felt extremely lonely. When pressed, she admitted, "I don't feel like anyone truly understands me." She also recognized that there were few people she truly felt close to. Frankly speaking, she felt lost. Nadine frequently questioned what life had to offer and whether this sense of isolation was inevitable.

Nadine had always struggled with feelings of loneliness. She speculated that her difficult childhood played a role. When her father abandoned the family, she was just 11 years old. Her mother was deeply traumatized, leaving Nadine to care for both her younger brother and her depressed mother.

DOI: 10.4324/9781003651260-10

She felt there was no one she could truly rely on, which led to a belief that her life didn't matter to others. Given her troubled upbringing, it was unsurprising that Nadine developed a rather pessimistic view of life.

Nadine entered the fashion industry hoping to build relationships. However, the reality turned out to be quite different. Despite the glamorous setting, her workplace was cutthroat, demanding a tough exterior just to survive. Nadine managed to claw her way up the ranks, but the environment fostered opportunistic alliances rather than meaningful friendships. This only exacerbated her negative view of humanity.

Loneliness is a form of loss that highlights the challenge of forging meaningful human connections.

Nadine's romantic life also left much to be desired. Her brief marriage ended in divorce, which she attributed to character incompatibility. Reflecting on it later, she saw the marriage as a miserable experience that made her even more wary of people. As a result, her subsequent romantic relationships were similarly short-lived.

Nadine's lifestyle prevented her from building real friendships, leaving her feeling profoundly lonely. Her loneliness often seemed to compound. After a hard day at work, Nadine had little energy to reach out, and her low self-esteem made establishing relationships even harder. Too embarrassed or ashamed to admit her loneliness, she kept it private. In her darker moments, she even imagined it stemmed from a personal inadequacy.

There were times, however, that Nadine thought it was much better to be alone, as she believed it prevented her from getting hurt. Yet, she also wondered if she had developed an aversion to people. She recognized that her loneliness led to frequent anxiety, depressive thoughts, and, despite her denial, her struggles with alcohol. Resigned to her fate, Nadine was convinced that loneliness was her destiny and that no one would ever love her.

THE LONELINESS CONUNDRUM

The English poet John Donne famously wrote, "No man is an island," while the American playwright Tennessee Williams remarked that "We are all sentenced to solitary confinement inside our own skins, for life."[3] Despite these seemingly opposing perspectives, it's clear that humans need social connections to thrive. Without them, we experience a sense of loss. Loneliness is often intensified by the death of a loved one—a theme that will be explored in Chapters 13, 14, and 15. When someone close to us dies, they leave a void that nothing can fill. In this chapter, however, we focus on existential loneliness and the feelings of loss that come with it.

Loneliness is defined as the distressing emotional state that arises when there is a gap between the relationships we desire and those we actually have.

Throughout history, writers, poets, and philosophers have extensively explored loneliness. It is defined as the distressing emotional state that arises when there is a gap between the relationships we desire and those we actually have. Loneliness stems from feeling our connections are inadequate or unfulfilling, leading to a sense of exclusion, isolation, and a lack of intimacy. This isolation is often intensified by feelings of rejection or abandonment.

It is worth noting that loneliness is subjective. We can have many connections and still feel lonely. Some people feel deeply alone in a crowd, with friends, or even in a marriage. Clearly, loneliness is not just about the number of connections but their quality. While some may feel lonely when alone, others may be perfectly happy spending significant time on their own.

It is worth noting that loneliness is subjective. We can have many connections and still feel lonely.

Solitude

Feelings of loneliness differ from solitude. As the German-American philosopher Paul Tillich acutely noted, "Loneliness expresses the pain of being alone and solitude expresses the glory of being alone."[4] Some people enjoy solitude without feeling lonely at all. These individuals enjoy their own company while still maintaining positive social relationships they can turn to when they feel the need to connect. They engage socially but balance it with time alone.

For these individuals, the silence of solitude helps them stay connected with themselves. At times, it's essential to take a break from others and enjoy "me time." Spending time alone allows the mind to refresh. In fact, solitude can serve as a gateway to original thought and creativity.

Solitude can serve as a gateway to original thought and creativity.

A SEARCH FOR ORIGINS

The questions remain: Why does loneliness impact people so deeply? Why is it such an important theme? Why does it create a sense of being lost?

The evolutionary point of view

Humans are wired for social connection. The need to belong is as fundamental as the need for water, food, and shelter. *Homo sapiens* thrived in social settings because we are born helpless, dependent on care for far longer than other primates. Therefore, it is unsurprising that the human brain, having evolved to seek safety in numbers, registers loneliness as a major threat. For our Paleolithic ancestors, isolation meant great danger. In such situations, the brain's threat-monitoring system, including the amygdala, triggers a "fight or flight" response, releasing stress hormones. This behavioral pattern indicates that humans rely on safe social surroundings to survive and thrive. Loneliness, then, is a helpful and adaptive response, motivating us to reconnect with others—a vital mechanism for survival.

> Loneliness is a helpful and adaptive response, motivating us to reconnect with others—a vital mechanism for survival.

The psychodynamic-systemic perspective

From a psychodynamic-systemic perspective, these reactions underscore the importance of developmental processes, particularly basic attachment behavior. Here, we refer to the bio-social bond between caregiver and infant. Infants need a relationship with at least one "good enough" primary caregiver for healthy emotional and social development. This biologically driven need for intimacy persists throughout life. Attachment bonds can be secure, anxious, or avoidant. If the early attachment process is dysfunctional—lacking a strong emotional bond between infant and caregiver—it affects future relationships. Traumatic attachment patterns can lead to intimacy issues and a lasting sense of loss. In other words, if primary caretakers fail to establish a secure base, it becomes difficult for the infant and later the adult to establish close relationships. Dysfunctional attachment can result from parenting style, traditions, mental health issues (including personality disorders), or abusive family environments.

Children with insecure attachment patterns often behave in ways that lead to rejection by peers, hindering their social development. They tend to be pessimistic or even hostile in social interactions. This lays the groundwork for lasting feelings of loneliness. At the core of loneliness is a deep and powerful yearning for connection with a lost self. It is a longing for an attachment relationship that never materialized, resulting in discomfort with themselves and others. Thus, attachment relationships during critical early stages of development determine feelings of belonging, integration into social networks, and participation in community life.[5]

> At the core of loneliness is a deep and powerful
> yearning for connection with a lost self.

THE MANY COLORS OF LONELINESS

Loneliness can be expressed in various ways. Some people withdraw, whereas others become irritable or angry. Typically, the lonely tend to avoid social events and feel apprehensive about engaging with others. They may feel overwhelmed in busy public places, work events, or parties. They may also find it hard to try new things. Nadine's experience is a good example: she found it difficult—and even shameful—to share her feelings. These individuals fear that they won't be understood and worry about burdening others with their concerns.

Transient versus chronic loneliness

Most of us will experience loneliness at some point; it's part of being human. Occasional loneliness isn't necessarily a bad thing. In fact, it can even be considered a healthy response—a mental signal urging us to strengthen our social connections. This sense of loss serves as a warning sign that our lives may have become unbalanced.

There can be many causes for this mental state, from overworking to moving, or, more dramatically, the loss of a loved one. In these moments, loneliness can remind us that action is needed, highlighting our fundamental need for connection. These feelings may motivate us to strengthen existing relationships or seek new ones.

> Occasional loneliness isn't necessarily a bad thing. In fact,
> it can even be considered a healthy response—a mental
> signal urging us to strengthen our social connections.

In small doses, loneliness—like hunger or thirst—acts as a healthy signal that something essential is missing. It forces us to reflect and may help us redefine what truly matters. However, when loneliness becomes chronic, it can lead to negative mental and physical health outcomes.

Chronic loneliness, as seen with Nadine, is harmful because it doesn't prompt constructive action. While transient loneliness typically motivates people to improve their relationships, chronic loneliness leads to greater inaction. It often creates hypervigilance about others' motives, fostering a destructive cycle of negativity and distrust. This mindset fuels cynicism and suspicion, hindering the creation of positive relationships. In this regard, chronic loneliness can become self-reinforcing. It has been linked to higher risks of depression, dementia, self-harm, and suicide.[6] Ultimately, those struggling with chronic loneliness don't have a good relationship with themselves.

Chronic loneliness is harmful because it doesn't prompt constructive action. While transient loneliness typically motivates people to improve their relationships, chronic loneliness leads to greater inaction.

Interpersonal loneliness

Apart from differentiating transient and chronic loneliness, there's interpersonal loneliness, which is the type of loneliness most referenced and portrayed in the media. People experiencing this form feel socially isolated, lack intimate relationships, and believe they have no real friends or trustworthy connections. As mentioned earlier, personality factors related to attachment patterns contribute to these feelings. In essence, interpersonal loneliness is deeply personal, rooted in a person's character and their inability to form meaningful connections with others.

Interpersonal loneliness is deeply personal, rooted in a person's character and their inability to form meaningful connections with others.

Contextual loneliness

To these various conceptualizations, we can also add contextual loneliness. This refers to societal exclusion, a situation whereby individuals feel systemically excluded due to specific characteristics or backgrounds. Individuals experiencing contextual loneliness may lack a wider social network or sense of community, feeling alienated from mainstream culture. It disproportionately affects minorities and underserved groups, and is related to the loss or lack of a social identity.[7] Prejudiced attitudes and discriminatory practices exacerbate this type of loneliness. However, it extends beyond race, class, and gender, affecting anyone systemically excluded—such as those who don't fit mainstream beauty standards, people with disabilities, and even the elderly.

> Contextual loneliness refers to societal exclusion, a situation whereby individuals feel systemically excluded due to specific characteristics or backgrounds.

Existential loneliness

Existential loneliness is tied to profound questions like "Does my life have meaning?" "Is there a purpose to my life?" "How do I fit into the universe?" "Why do I feel this loss?" It underpins much spiritual and religious work. It differs from lacking companionship or being systemically excluded. But existential loneliness is an inevitable part of the human condition—we come into the world alone, journey through life individually, and die alone. In essence, existential loneliness is rooted in the paradox between our search for meaning and the vast isolation of the universe. Fears related to mortality, such as disappearing, being forgotten, or dying, are closely intertwined with this type of loneliness.

> Existential loneliness is rooted in the paradox between our search for meaning and the vast isolation of the universe.

LIVING IN DYSTOPIA

We are all born alone and die alone, making loneliness perhaps our greatest fear, whether we realize it or not. As an inevitable part of the human condition, loneliness is woven into the fabric of life. It has been and always will be central to the experience of every human being. Yet, the eternal quest is to overcome this loneliness, a pursuit that has grown increasingly difficult in modern society.

> We are all born alone and die alone, making loneliness perhaps our greatest fear, whether we realize it or not.

We live in a kind of dystopia, where technology fuels alienation. Another factor contributing to loneliness today is that we have become more mobile than ever before. This has driven us away from the communities we grew up with and got to know over time. As a result, many live a transient life, rife with loneliness and rootlessness. Despite being more connected than ever through technology, many people still feel isolated, lacking meaningful relationships. This creates a paradox where we gather, yet still feel alone—a troubling consequence of modern life.

Today, we live in a kind of dystopia, where technology fuels alienation.

It has taken a long time for loneliness to be taken seriously and for us truly to understand its impact. Despite affecting so many, loneliness has received far less attention than related conditions such as depression or anxiety. It often goes unrecognized, even among people we know quite well. Loneliness can lead to a downward spiral, intensifying a sense of loss. It's crucial to remember that loneliness profoundly impacts both mental and physical health.

Being alone is something few of us can handle. Everyone desires relationships and community. The eternal quest to overcome loneliness is both natural and deeply human. After all, while loneliness has the potential to harm, connection holds the power to heal.

The eternal quest to overcome loneliness is both natural
and deeply human. After all, while loneliness has the
potential to harm, connection holds the power to heal.

NOTES

1   Thomas De Quincey (1851/1845). The affliction of childhood. In *Suspiria de Profundis—A Sequel to Confessions of an English Opium-Eater*. Boston, MA: Ticknor and Fields.

2   Michel de Montaigne (1947/1580). Of solitude. In *The Essays of Michel de Montaigne*. Trans. George B. Ives. New York: The Heritage Press, Volume I, Chapter XXXIX, p. 323.

3   John Donne (2015/1624). From: XVII. Meditation. Devotions upon emergent occasions. In *The Complete John Donne*. Bybliotech.

4   Paraphrased from Paul Tillich (1963). Loneliness and solitude. In *The Eternal Now*. New York: Charles Scribner's Sons, Part One, Chapter 1, pp. 17–18.

5   John Bowlby (1983). *Attachment: Attachment and Loss, Volume One*. New York: Basic Books.

6   Raheel Mushtaq, Sheikh Shoib, Tabindah Shah, and Sahil Mushtaq (2014). Relationship between loneliness, psychiatric disorders and physical health: A review on the psychological aspects of loneliness. *Journal of Clinical and Diagnostic Research*, 8(9), 1–4.

7   Natalie Cotterell, Tine Buffel, James Nazroo, and Pamela Qualter (2025). Loneliness among older ethnic minority people: Exploring the role of structural disadvantage and place using a co-research methodology. *Ethnic and Racial Studies*, 48(1), 206–228.

9

A PRESENT-DAY PANDEMIC

When, musing on companions gone,
We doubly feel ourselves alone.

—Sir Walter Scott[1]

The strongest man in the world is he who stands most alone.

—Henrik Ibsen[2]

THE LONELINESS PANDEMIC

To continue exploring the theme of loneliness, let's look at contemporary society and the growing forces driving us apart. As Nadine's case illustrated, we can feel lonely even when surrounded by people. Paradoxically, despite our increased connectivity through technology and social media, the experience of loneliness persists and even grows, creating a sense of loss that is hard to quantify.

Social media can unite people with shared interests, yet it also amplifies disagreement and creates divisive echo chambers. Scrolling through curated images often intensifies the feeling of missing out, deepening loneliness. Despite having many followers or online connections, people may not feel truly known or supported in times of need. Instead, these online communities can become havens for loneliness.

> The lonelier we feel, the more it shapes our thought
> processes, making feelings of loss harder to overcome.

DOI: 10.4324/9781003651260-11

As Nadine's story showed, the lonelier we feel, the more it shapes our thought processes, making feelings of loss harder to overcome. While strong, supportive networks are crucial for our well-being, our modern world is grappling with a pandemic of loneliness, which was exacerbated during the Covid-19 pandemic. Loneliness has turned into a modern-day malaise—a silent plague or invisible affliction.

Given its destructive nature, the loneliness pandemic must be recognized for its serious consequences on mental, physical, and collective well-being. Leaders should make greater efforts to address the widespread isolation many face. It warrants the same level of attention as other public health issues such as smoking, drinking, drug abuse, and obesity.

Loneliness has turned into a modern-day
malaise—a silent plague or invisible affliction.

Contributing factors

Crucial questions arise: Why does loneliness haunt us? Why do we experience this sense of loss? Why are we in this situation? A major factor is societal transformation. In today's world, constant change has become the norm, and many of these shifts have weakened our ability to connect with others.

From a social organizational perspective, we've observed a shift from *Gemeinschaft* to *Gesellschaft*, concepts introduced by German sociologist Ferdinand Tönnies. *Gemeinschaft* refers to communal, rural societies where personal relationships are guided by tradition, while *Gesellschaft* describes more impersonal, cosmopolitan societies.[3] In *Gesellschaft*-oriented environments, opportunities for deep social connections are diminished.

In today's world, constant change has become the norm, and many
of these shifts have weakened our ability to connect with others.

The shift from *Gemeinschaft* to *Gesellschaft* has been marked by rapid industrialization, the growth of the consumer economy, materialism, and the declining influence of religion, all amplified by the rise of social media. In these impersonal societies, barriers between neighbors have grown, fueled by identity politics, racial divides, and class disparities. All of this has compounded feelings of isolation and loneliness. In addition, household sizes have shrunk as extended families give way to nuclear ones. For the first time in human history, many people across all demographics are choosing to live alone. High divorce rates, falling birth rates, and longer lifespans—especially among women outliving their husbands—have also contributed to this increase in single-person households.

> For the first time in human history, many people across all demographics are choosing to live alone.

In the past, people stayed rooted in one place due to localized employment. Nowadays, frequent job changes and relocations often separate individuals from family and friends. Additionally, the widespread use of technology has profoundly changed how we work and interact. The rapid rise of remote work and associated technologies has disrupted meaningful face-to-face connections, leaving many people feeling lost.

In addition to societal changes, personal factors such as illness, disability, employment status, financial issues, retirement, divorce, or the loss of a loved one can contribute to loneliness. For instance, illness or disability can alter self-perception and relationships, leading to isolation. Unemployment may bring embarrassment, while financial problems can cause shame, identity loss, and considerable stress. Retirement and divorce often result in the loss of support networks, deepening loneliness. Naturally, the death of a loved one also brings a profound sense of isolation.

> The rapid rise of remote work and associated technologies has disrupted meaningful face-to-face connections, leaving many people feeling lost.

Migrants are another demographic particularly prone to loneliness, which often stems from a loss or lack of a social identity. Their inability to identify with or belong to the more "valued" societal groups limits access to social and psychological resources, including being part of a social network.

As we saw with Nadine, chronic loneliness tends to be more intrapsychic, rooted in a person's developmental history and leading to low self-esteem. People like Nadine often feel unworthy of attention or respect, which further intensifies their chronic loneliness.

> Chronic loneliness tends to be more intrapsychic, rooted in a person's developmental history and leading to low self-esteem.

Some figures

It is estimated that one in two people experiences measurable loneliness. One study found that 9 percent of adults in Japan, 22 percent in America, and 23 percent in Britain often or always feel lonely, lack companionship, or feel isolated.[4] Factors such as gender, marital status, and age influence loneliness. Women, for example, may be more willing to express loneliness, though they may not feel it more than men. Married or cohabiting individuals tend to experience less loneliness. Having a partner appears to be especially important for older adults, as they generally have fewer but closer relationships. However, there's no clear link between age and loneliness overall, which can occur at any stage of life.[5] Young adults, for instance, often face uncertainties around relationships, career choices, and independence, all of which can contribute to feelings of loneliness.

It is estimated that one in two people experiences measurable loneliness.

PHYSICAL AND MENTAL HEALTH ISSUES

The impact of the loneliness pandemic on mental, physical, and societal well-being is undeniable. Chronic stress from loneliness can keep the body in a perpetual low-level fight-or-flight mode, causing serious wear and tear. Physically, loneliness increases the risk of heart disease, stroke, and, particularly among older adults, dementia. Some claim loneliness kills more people than cancer, while others compare its mortality risk with smoking 15 cigarettes a day or being an alcoholic.[6]

Some claim loneliness kills more people than cancer, while others compare its mortality risk with smoking 15 cigarettes a day or being an alcoholic.

Beyond physical health, loneliness and isolation significantly impact mental health. Prolonged loneliness can spur depressive reactions, increasing the risk of premature death. It may also lead to unhealthy behaviors like eating disorders, drug abuse, smoking, or alcoholism. It can also result in sleep deprivation and prolonged feelings of anxiety. Lonely people may be less motivated to seek preventive care, adhere to medication, or practice self-care. The relationship between loneliness and ill health is reciprocal: loneliness leads to ill health, and vice versa.

It's no surprise, then, that those who live to a ripe old age often exhibit positive health behaviors, including strong social connections. The ability to connect with others—and the physical and psychological benefits of connection—enables them to live longer lives. Reduced loneliness is associated with a greater chance of living longer.[7]

The relationship between loneliness and ill health is reciprocal:
loneliness leads to ill health, and vice versa.

Loneliness also affects our ability to work effectively. For example, younger people who grappled with loneliness and isolation during the Covid-19 pandemic found it very difficult to focus on their schoolwork or perform well in their jobs. Similarly, older adults who experience loneliness are more likely to feel unwell at work and may struggle to perform efficiently or to the best of their abilities.[8]

WHAT CAN BE DONE ABOUT IT?

While the loneliness pandemic is widespread and has weighty consequences for individual and collective well-being, the obvious antidote is fostering social connection and community. Although loneliness can be destructive, forming connections is deeply healing. Perhaps one of the most constructive outcomes of the Covid-19 pandemic is that it has highlighted our need for interconnectedness. Despite the anxiety, fear, and uncertainty the pandemic brought, it also underscored the importance of effective coping strategies to promote well-being and mental health.

Although loneliness can be destructive, forming connections is deeply healing.

Societal considerations

To be truly healthy, happy, and fulfilled, we may need to rethink how we interact with others. We can begin by prioritizing social connection and self-care, while being more intentional about ensuring our social needs are met. A society where people are more connected tends to fare better in terms of public health, safety, resilience, civic engagement, and prosperity.[9]

To be truly healthy, happy, and fulfilled, we may need to rethink
how we interact with others.

Several societal interventions can help foster a culture of connection. We need more policies, strategies, and programs that prioritize connectivity to help people overcome their sense of loss. This may involve reassessing our relationship with technology to ensure digital interactions enhance, rather than detract from, meaningful connections. Leaders should design social infrastructures that facilitate connection, such as investing in public transportation, parks, community centers, and libraries. Creating living communities that encourage social interaction is another option. Most importantly, we must build a society that values connection and places civility at its core.

We must build a society that values connection and places civility at its core.

A personal perspective

On a personal level, we all have the power to address the loss that loneliness brings. Often, we are lonely because we build walls instead of bridges. As the American short story writer and journalist, Ambroise Bierce, wisely defined it: "ALONE, *adj.* In bad company."[10] Spending time alone, however, can be a valuable growth experience. Loneliness offers an opportunity for introspection and self-understanding. At times, it may be helpful to carve out mental space to re-examine our lives. Learning to be comfortable with solitude can ultimately enhance our ability to form meaningful, intimate relationships.

Often, we are lonely because we build walls instead of bridges.
Learning to be comfortable with solitude can ultimately enhance our ability to form meaningful, intimate relationships.

If we use our solitude wisely, we can gain greater self-awareness. This may help us better understand why we do what we do. Loneliness can push us out of our comfort zones and prompt a journey of self-discovery that we might otherwise avoid in our busy lives. It offers a pause to reflect on our inner thoughts and understand why we feel isolated.

Loneliness can push us out of our comfort zones and prompt a journey of self-discovery that we might otherwise avoid in our busy lives. It offers a pause to reflect on our inner thoughts and understand why we feel isolated.

Besides self-reflection, there are steps we can take to address loneliness:

- *Reach out.* When feeling lonely, it's crucial to reach out to our networks, even if we're hesitant. Connecting with family and friends—via phone, email, or social media—can ease the burden of loneliness. Strengthening current relationships might be as simple as reconnecting with someone we haven't spoken to in a while.
- *Build new connections.* We should also make an effort to build new connections. While this may be challenging, especially as we age, the benefits are substantial. Expanding our social circles can be done by joining interest-based groups, becoming involved in professional organizations, or attending conferences. Ultimately, we must invest in our social well-being.

Ultimately, we must invest in our social well-being.

- *Embracing online communities.* Online communities can be valuable refuges during bouts of loneliness. Creating a Meetup group for people with similar interests is one way to foster connections. Despite its drawbacks, the Internet is home to many groups that allow instant connection from the comfort of home. Participating in support groups, WhatsApp forums, or online chat groups can offer a safe, supportive space to connect with others experiencing similar emotions.
- *Non-human companions.* Although it sounds out of the ordinary, having a companion animal can also significantly alleviate loneliness. Pets provide constant companionship, comfort, and unconditional love, which can have therapeutic effects on mental health.[11] Petting an animal releases oxytocin, the "love hormone," promoting well-being and a positive mood. In addition, caring for a pet encourages daily routines, such as going outside, which can lead to interactions with others and facilitate conversations.

Caring for a pet encourages daily routines, such as going outside, which can lead to interactions with others and facilitate conversations.

- *Helping others.* While seeking support is commonly seen as the best remedy for loneliness, managing these feelings should not be one-directional. It's not just about receiving attention but also giving it. Reaching out to help others, though initially challenging, can be highly effective. Intentional acts of kindness and generosity boost our sense of self-worth and break down feelings of isolation. Community service or similar altruistic activities provide opportunities to meet people, form new friendships, and find a sense of purpose. Regularly practicing gratitude and altruism can shift a mindset that views new encounters as threats.

Regularly practicing gratitude and altruism can shift a mindset that views new encounters as threats.

- *Seek professional help.* If previous efforts haven't eased loneliness, it may be time to seek professional help. A therapist can help address low self-esteem and negative thought patterns that hinder meaningful relationships. Hopeful thinking and planning for the future can encourage efforts to connect with others. Whether through individual therapy or group interventions, a mental health professional can offer valuable guidance. Online therapy is also a convenient option. It's important to recognize that, like any medical condition, loneliness can worsen if left untreated.

It's important to recognize that, like any medical condition, loneliness can worsen if left untreated.

THE PRISON OF HUMAN EXPERIENCE

Throughout history, loneliness has been a constant and significant experience. It is undeniably one of the most daunting experiences, as it can feel like being imprisoned within oneself. When a person feels trapped in this emotional prison, despair can swiftly follow.

Loneliness is undeniably one of the most daunting experiences, as it can feel like being imprisoned within oneself.

For many, learning to be alone without feeling lonely is a challenge. Even those in committed relationships or with active social lives will feel lonely at times. This sense of loss is common. Fortunately, for most, it's transient, simply part of life's natural ebb and flow. However, loneliness can spiral when fueled by trauma, illness, loss, aging, or the replacement of human interaction with technology. Undoubtedly, all of us need a social circle and intimate connections to navigate life's complexities.

For many, learning to be alone without feeling lonely is a challenge.

When experiencing loneliness, it's crucial to avoid self-blame, as it only perpetuates shame, low self-esteem, and guilt. This mindset may discourage us from reaching out to others. While personality traits contribute to loneliness, social and cultural factors play a key role too. Accepting that loneliness is a universal part of the human experience, like hunger or thirst, can offer a more constructive perspective.

When experiencing loneliness, it's crucial to avoid self-blame, as it only perpetuates shame, low self-esteem, and guilt.

Despite affecting many, loneliness doesn't receive the attention given to other disorders, and this needs to change. We must make more of a conscious effort to combat loneliness, considering its harmful effects on well-being and behavior. However, we shouldn't expect things to change overnight. Like many endeavors, altering our perspective takes time and patience.

As a closing reflection, I view loneliness not only as a warning sign but also as a blessing in disguise—a chance for personal growth. A sense of loss can be a catalyst for change. Loneliness arises not from a lack of people, but from an inability to share what truly matters. The shock death of the American actor and comedian Robin Williams acts as a reminder, with the Internet community using Rorschach's (from *Watchmen*) 'joke' after the death of the vigilante The Comedian as a poignant tribute:

> I heard a joke once. Man goes to doctor, says he's depressed. Life seems harsh and cruel. Says he feels all alone in a threatening world where what lies ahead is vague and uncertain. Doctor says, 'Treatment is simple. The great clown, Pagliacci, is in town. Go see him. That should pick you up.' Man bursts into tears. 'But Doctor,' he says, 'I am Pagliacci.' Good joke. Everybody laugh. Roll on snare drum. Curtains.[12]

Everyone handles this sense of loss differently, and healing can only begin when we fully acknowledge the loss.

Loneliness arises not from a lack of people, but from an inability to share what truly matters.

NOTES

1 Sir Walter Scott (1893/1808). Introduction to Canto Second. In *Marmion*. Ed. William J. Rolfe. Boston, MA and New York: Houghton, Mifflin and Company.

2 Henrik Ibsen (1917/1882). An enemy of the people. In *Ghosts, and Other Plays*. Trans. R. Farquharson Sharp. London: Dent, Act V.

3 Ferdinand Tönnies (2017/1887). *Gemeinschaft und Gesellschaft*. München/Wien: Profil-Verlag.

4 The Data Team (2018). Loneliness is pervasive and rising, particularly among the young. *The Economist*. www.economist.com/graphic-detail/2018/08/31/loneliness-is-pervasive-and-rising-particu larly-among-the-young

5 Keming Yang and Christina Victor (2011). Age and loneliness in 25 European nations. *Ageing & Society*, *31*(8), 1368–1388. https://doi.org/10.1017/S0144686X1000139X

6 John D. Cacioppo, L. Elizabeth Crawford, Louise Hawkley, and John Ernst (2002). Loneliness and health: Potential mechanisms. *Psychosomatic Medicine*, *64*(3), 407–417; Julianne Holt-Lunstad, Timothy B. Smith, and Tyler Harris (2015). Loneliness and social isolation as risk factors for mortality: A meta-analytic review. *Perspectives on Psychological Science*, *10*(2), 227–237; Julianne Holt-Lunstad (2017). The potential public health relevance of social isolation and loneliness: Prevalence, epidemiology, and risk factors. *Public Policy & Aging Report*, *27*(4), 127–130; Nicole K. Valtorta, Mona Kanaan, Simon Gilbody, Sara Ronzi, and Barbara Hanratty (2016). Loneliness and social isolation as risk factors for coronary heart disease and stroke: Systematic review and meta-analysis of longitudinal observational studies. *Heart*, *102*(13), 1009–1016. https://doi.org/10.1136/heartjnl-2015-308790

7 Cacioppo, Crawford, Hawkley, and Ernst, Loneliness and health; Holt-Lunstad, Smith, Harris, Loneliness and social isolation as risk factors for mortality; Holt-Lunstad, The potential public health relevance of social isolation and loneliness; Valtorta, Kanaan, Gilbody, Ronzi, and Hanratty, Loneliness and social isolation as risk factors for coronary heart disease and stroke.

8 Hakan Ozcelik and Sigal Barsade (2018). No employee an island: Workplace loneliness and job performance. *Academy of Management Journal*, *61*(6), 2343–2366. https://doi.org/10.5465/amj.2015.1066

9 Julianne Holt-Lunstad, Timothy B. Smith, and J. Bradley Layton (2010). Social relationships and mortality risk: A meta-analytic review. *PLOS Medicine*. https://doi.org/10.1371/journal.pmed.1000316

10 Ambrose Bierce (1906). *The Cynic's Word Book*. New York: Doubleday, Page & Company.

11 UCLA Health (2025). Animal Assisted Therapy & What Science Says. www.uclahealth.org/programs/pac/about-us/animal-assisted-therapy-research

12 Kevin McFarland (2014, 12 August). Remembering Robin Williams, cinema's Rorschach test. BOING BOING. https://boingboing.net/2014/08/12/remembering-robin-williams-ci.html [Video]

10

SEX AND THE EXECUTIVE

The behavior of a human being in sexual matters is often a prototype for the whole of his other modes of reaction to life.

—Sigmund Freud[1]

Of all sexual aberrations, chastity is the strangest.

—Remy de Gourmont[2]

There are various ways to combat loneliness, and, as we've seen, these methods can effectively address this sense of loss. Some people, struggling with direction in life, may engage in what can be described as "manic" sexual activities, yet they often fail to form truly intimate relationships. Obsessive sexual behavior seems to become their way of coping with life's challenges, as illustrated in Leonardo's case.

"Monogamy is boring, but serial monogamy can be quite expensive," Leonardo muttered as he settled into his seat on a plane bound for London. He had to admit, his sexual escapades were not exactly the cheapest form of entertainment. Officially, the trip was for a business meeting, but the real reason was yet another sexual adventure. Even though Leonardo seemed to have it all—wife, children, dogs, sports cars, and a beautiful summer house in Tuscany—he felt unsatisfied. Restless for reasons he couldn't explain, he convinced himself that life without sexual adventures would be unbearably dull. This sense of boredom extended to his relationship with his wife.

At times, Leonardo wondered if he had only got married because it was expected. Looking back, he convinced himself that he wasn't really the

DOI: 10.4324/9781003651260-12

marrying type. His marriage, he realized, had morphed into more of a sibling relationship. Whatever sexual desire he once had for his wife had long dissipated. Rarely did the two of them have any physical contact. If sex was the barometer of their marriage, it had stopped functioning long ago.

The occasional sex felt like two drowning people trying to save each other.

Leonardo had concluded that domestic eroticism wasn't for him. He had very little to say to the person who once shared his bed so prominently. If he was honest with himself, he no longer liked to sleep in the same bed as his wife, and the occasional sex felt like two drowning people trying to save each other. Despite how his marriage had turned out, divorce was out of the question—too much of a hassle, and life was too comfortable. Unlike some of his friends, he preferred to live with the status quo. Leonardo recalled once suggesting an open marriage, but his wife's reaction made it clear it wasn't her cup of tea. Secret affairs, then, were easier and more convenient.

Leonardo had also realized that watching porn and fantasizing about bondage or sadomasochism alone wasn't enough. It was a one-man show that failed to satisfy. He needed more and, fortunately, he had found other ways to get his fix. A lucky break had led him to a high-class brothel in Soho, courtesy of an acquaintance, and he'd become a regular.

Leonardo was pleased with how the hostesses catered to his fantasies. Despite the considerable cost, he felt it was well worth it. He always found it extremely exciting to enter the place—it was like being a kid in a candy store. He often felt a twinge of ambivalence before heading there, but a few strong drinks always took care of that. Alcohol had long been his way of shedding inhibitions.

Visiting the establishment wasn't without risk. Once, Leonardo had narrowly escaped a police raid, and the fear of being caught was always in the back of his mind. Such a scandal would be very embarrassing. Recently, his boss had asked why he needed to visit London so frequently. Wouldn't it be much more convenient (and far less expensive) to deal with some of these business issues virtually? Leonardo had emphasized the importance of face-to-face meetings, but his boss's words lingered. Could people at the company know what he was really up to? He thought he'd been clever by spreading out his expenses, but how long would his luck hold? Would the accounting department eventually catch on?

Leonardo vividly remembered how, in his previous job, he had been caught fiddling with his expense account to pay for his sexual adventures. Having to finally face the music had been a downer, to say the least, and he had been told to leave. Fortunately, his strong contributions to the company's bottom line allowed him to make an "elegant exit" after persuading the CEO not to pursue the matter further. It wasn't an incident he wanted to remember, especially as he had really liked working there. The situation was complicated by the white lies he had to tell his wife to explain his departure. The whole ordeal taught him he should have been more cautious, but he found himself repeating the same behavior. He just couldn't stop.

A therapist once suggested that his obsessive pursuit of sex could be a sign of distress, and that beneath his compulsions lay a deep desire to be loved.

So why couldn't he help himself? He recalled opening up to a psychotherapist he had met during his university studies. Something she said had stuck with him—he might be using sex to mask his insecurities. She suggested that his obsessive pursuit of sex could be a sign of distress, and that beneath his compulsions lay a deep desire to be loved. In fact, Leonardo came to understand that his behavior might be a desperate attempt to feel less lonely. The psychotherapist had asked, "If sex is everything to you, why do you always end up feeling sad and empty afterward?" He didn't have an answer.

Leonardo had to admit that sex with people he didn't care about only made him feel lonelier than before. No matter how often he had sex, it never assuaged his feelings. The psychotherapist made him realize that his sexual adventures neither quelled his desires nor satisfied him. She added that without mutual care, sex was merely a form of auto-arousal, devoid of intimacy and connection, and true satisfaction came from emotional bonding. She also pointed out that his compulsive pursuit of sex could be a sign of depression. What's more, his high turnover of sexual partners might leave him emotionally stunted.

Without mutual care, sex was merely a form of auto-arousal, devoid of intimacy and connection, and true satisfaction came from emotional bonding.

This discussion made Leonardo realize that real intimacy might scare him. His compulsive need for sex was a form of self-medication—a way to fight an inner deadness. This was why he felt compelled to repeat his sexual adventures; it was his way of feeling alive.

The topic of online pornography also came up. His university acquaintance had also said that those obsessed with it often discover sexual possibilities they hadn't imagined. The danger, according to the psychotherapist, was that such explorations were creating unrealistic expectations for real-life encounters. Once again, Leonardo had to admit she had struck a nerve.

Leonardo remembered being encouraged by her to explore the reasons behind his behavior. When he hesitated, she emphasized the importance of understanding the origins of his compulsive sexuality if he wanted to deal with it. Why was he so compelled to act this way? Could it be a neurological issue, with certain neurotransmitters working overtime? Did his brain require more sexual stimulation than others to feel satisfied? Or could it be that he had experienced specific childhood traumas? Was there something in his family dynamics that could explain his condition?

His past could be an explanation why he sought out sex with anonymous partners; perhaps it freed him from the anxiety of being "invaded" and that of being abandoned.

Reflecting on the latter, Leonardo admitted that it hadn't helped having a father who never had a kind word for him. Their relationship was painful, and as a philanderer himself, his father wasn't exactly a role model. Then there was his mother, whom he remembered as cold and distant—someone he could never get close to. Leonardo's experiences with peers weren't much better. Many had tried to take advantage of him. Given how he'd been treated, it made sense that he concluded he couldn't rely on anyone and had to fend for himself.

Leonardo had always felt that being close to others was fraught with danger. No wonder he had relationship anxiety. His past could be an explanation why he sought out sex with anonymous partners; perhaps it freed him from the anxiety of being "invaded" and that of being abandoned. His sexual addiction was likely a way to avoid meaningful relationships. But the psychotherapist also pointed out that, in doing so, he was incomplete and missing out on important aspects of life. His "manic" sexual pursuits seemed to be a form of compensation for the loss of intimate connections.

In his pursuit of sexual highs, Leonardo came to understand they were merely a substitute for the support and intimacy that he really longed for but was afraid to experience. His sexual obsessions were propelled by the belief that using somebody else's body could alleviate his loneliness. It had become his way of coping with the emptiness inside and his sense of loss. In essence, he had an intimacy disorder—he was afraid of closeness. It made him wonder whether his fear of abandonment was only surpassed by his terror of intimacy. Could his sexual frenzy be masking a deeper emotional deficiency? Was it a way to deal with unresolved psychological problems? Unconsciously, he might have been looking for love, but this had manifested as frantic sexual activity.

His sexual obsessions were propelled by the belief that using somebody else's body could alleviate his loneliness.

Leonardo had to admit that deconstructing his obsessive need for sex made him feel uncomfortable, but deep down, he knew the psychotherapist might be right. The idea that he was developmentally stuck and that his manic sexual behavior was far from mature resonated with him. Perhaps his sexual activities weren't about intercourse, but rather a convoluted way of fulfilling his need for contact and communication. Perhaps it was his way of coping with the sense of loss he'd experienced while growing up.

The more Leonardo thought about it, the more uneasy he grew. He even wondered if he was waging some kind of "biological warfare" against his own body. Was he experiencing temporary psychotic episodes? The word psychosis crossed his mind because of the sense of unreality that accompanied his sexual activities. When he was visiting the brothel, it felt like he was losing touch with reality—entering a delusionary state where he lost his moral compass. He would do things that he deeply regretted afterward. What if his family and friends found out?

By indulging in sex whenever and with whomever he wanted, he had devalued it, rendering the act almost meaningless.

If Leonardo was truly honest, all his sexual encounters had blurred into nothingness. There had been so many nameless and faceless experiences. By indulging in sex whenever and with whomever he wanted, he had devalued it, rendering the act almost meaningless. Using sex outside its proper context not only hijacked his emotions but also exposed him to risks, like police raids or sexually transmitted diseases. The temporary relief sex provided seemed a poor counterweight to the stress it caused him.

Reflecting on his situation, Leonardo realized its precariousness. The truth was that he had a sex addiction and didn't know how to combat it. He often asked himself if life was worth living. Each morning, he woke up to fight the same demons that had left him so tired the day before. His addiction felt like a monster inside him, feeding on him, controlling him, and, if he wasn't careful, destined to destroy him. It was like life's perfect solvent: it could dissolve marriages, families, careers, and even lead to financial ruin. He was a lost soul, and if he continued on this path, he might end up losing everything.

> Sexual addiction was like life's perfect solvent: it could dissolve marriages, families, careers, and even lead to financial ruin.

NOTES

1   Sigmund Freud (1924/1908). "Civilized" sexual morality and modern nervousness. In *Collected Papers*. Trans. E. Herford and E. B. Colborn Mayne. London: Hogarth Press, Volume II.
2   Author's translation of the original: *De toutes les aberrations sexuelles, la plus singulière est peut-être encore la chasteté.* Remy de Gourmont (1903). La question des aberrations. In *La Physique de l'Amour: Essai sur l'Instinct Sexuel.* Paris: Société du Mercure de France, Chapter 1.

11

THE SEXUAL CONUNDRUM

As for sex, the last of the great words, it was just a cocktail term for an excitement that bucked you up for a while, then left you more raggy than ever. Frayed! It was as if the very material you were made of was cheap stuff, and was fraying out to nothing.

—D. H. Lawrence[1]

It is unfair of women to say that men only want sex. In reality, men are prone to two states: horny and hungry.

—Anon.

The key question for Leonardo, then, is how to address his sense of loss over intimacy, masked by his frantic sexual activity. Is there a way for him to live a more fulfilling life? Are there steps he can take?

For most people, sexual behavior doesn't cause any serious problems. Although their sexual journey may not always be smooth, they can find ways to integrate it into their lives. However, for people like Leonardo, sex may become a manic attempt to cope with the loss of intimacy by using the body to reconnect through physical sensations. For these individuals, sex becomes an obsession, one that haunts them endlessly. But this obsession might be masking deeper psychological issues, particularly related to how they handle intimacy and emotional connection.[2]

> For sex addicts, sex may become a manic attempt to cope with the loss of intimacy by using the body to reconnect through physical sensations.

DOI: 10.4324/9781003651260-13

Individuals like Leonardo confuse a loving relationship—marked by intimacy and care—with merely engaging in sexual acts. They fail to see the difference: being sensual relates to making love, while being sexual simply means having sex. They don't recognize that sex is only part of a relationship, nor do they appreciate that making love involves more than physical alignment. Sensuality is broader than sexuality: it has to do with the overall quality of a person's relationship with the other. It's about truly experiencing the partner's presence during the encounter. Many people have sex, but not as many make love. If someone views a relationship as strictly sexual, they miss out on truly sensual experiences. As life moved on, Leonardo was losing out on intimate relationships.

> Sensuality is broader than sexuality: it has to do with the
> overall quality of a person's relationship with the other.

For sex addicts, only the physical act seems to matter, while the intimacy and care that contribute to a truly sensual experience are foreign to them. Their focus is on the physiological responses to sexual stimulation, with the primary goal being orgasmic release. They attempt to replace what they lack in sensuality with sexuality, prioritizing physical gratification. Sex addicts don't understand that when people are deeply connected emotionally, sensuality and sexuality intertwine. It can become an extremely satisfactory, transcending experience. For sex addicts, however, their obsessive need for another "fix" shows that their sexual encounters fail to satisfy and only deepen their sense of loss.

This condition has been given many names: hypersexuality, hypersexual disorder, sexual compulsivity, sexual impulsivity, and sexual addiction disorder. From a gender-specific perspective, males with this condition have been described as having Don Juan syndrome, satyriasis, or priapism, whereas terms like clitoromaniac, nymphomaniac, and andromaniac have been used for females.

> Sex addicts don't understand that when people are deeply
> connected emotionally, sensuality and sexuality intertwine.

The behavior of a typical sex addict includes a wide variety of sexual activities such as the compulsive use of pornography, cybersex, frequent use of prostitutes, sexual massages, escorts, multiple affairs, anonymous sex, and compulsive masturbation. While many of these practices occur in people's sex lives, they become signs of addiction when sexual thoughts and actions dominate a person's life. In Leonardo's case, it's important to note that sex addicts often use these activities to manage underlying emotional conflicts.

Sexually obsessed people behave in a similar way to those who have substance-abuse problems. Just as people with alcohol or opiate addictions crave a repeated "fix," sex addicts experience a compulsive need for sexual gratification, much like the dependence seen in substance abuse.

> Sexually obsessed people behave in a similar way
> to those who have substance-abuse problems.

Culturally, this condition has been exacerbated by the rise of the Internet, which provides easy access to sexual services through dating sites, classified ads, and discussion boards. In fact, the Internet has made it easier for sex addicts to find outlets that feed their compulsions.

Despite the stress they experience, sex addicts seem unable to stop, control, or change their behavior. When opportunities for sex arise, they often enter a trancelike state, blocking out potential consequences. Like substance addicts, they persist in destructive behaviors regardless of the fallout, acting as if on autopilot. They continue despite the clear damage to their relationships, finances, careers, health, and even the legal risks of soliciting sex workers.

In the context of sex addiction, it's important to remember that sexual behavior is a normal and healthy part of life. Sexuality varies widely between individuals, and different activities appeal to different people, influenced by personal and cultural factors. Some are monogamous, while others prefer multiple partners or varied experiences. Sexual inclinations only become problematic when they cause significant distress or put individuals and others at risk of harm.

> Sexual inclinations only become problematic when they cause
> significant distress or put individuals and others at risk of harm.

THE DIFFICULTY OF DIAGNOSIS

When assessing sexual addiction, the following questions can be helpful, most of which would be answered in the affirmative by the typical sex addict:

- Do you feel overly distracted by, obsessed with, or preoccupied by your sexual fantasies and behavior?
- Is it very difficult for you to resist the urge to engage in sexual behaviors?

- Does pornography consume a considerable amount of your time?
- Do you need greater variety, frequency, or more extreme sexual activities to achieve the same excitement or relief?
- Do you rely on sex to reduce stress, anxiety, or boredom?
- Do sexual fantasies interfere with your ability to concentrate on tasks?
- Do you live a double life, feeling a need to keep secrets about your sexual behavior?
- Does your preoccupation with sex disrupt your family, social life, or work?
- Do you feel remorse, guilt, or shame after sexual activities?
- Do casual or anonymous encounters prevent you from forming long-term intimate relationships?

The diagnostic criteria for sex addiction remain vague and quite subjective. The paucity of empirical research and consensus validating specific sexual behavior as an addiction explains why it was excluded from the fifth edition of the *Diagnostic and Statistical Manual of Mental Disorders*. Despite this, sex addiction is still a valid concern in psychology and counseling due to its significant negative societal consequences.[3] Notably, the World Health Organization's *International Classification of Diseases* (ICD-11) includes compulsive sexual behavior disorder as a diagnosis.[4] Some researchers view the disorder as an issue of behavior regulating, whereas others suggest it stems from a higher sex drive or impulse control problems.

> Although research about sex addiction remains limited
> due to people's reluctance to discuss the topic, it
> appears to be more common than most people realize.

Although research about sex addiction remains limited due to people's reluctance to discuss the topic, it appears to be more common than most people realize. Estimates suggest that 3 percent to 6 percent of the general adult population in the United States suffer from sex addiction. Some studies even indicate an upper range of 10 percent. Also, around 80 percent of sex addicts are men.[5] However, the secretive nature of the issue makes assessing its global prevalence difficult. Identifying a compulsive sexual disorder is equally challenging due to the sensitive and personal nature of the behaviors. People rarely volunteer information about their condition, and the physical and psychological signs tend to be subtle or hidden. Without large epidemiological studies, the exact prevalence remains speculative.[6] Cultural factors also complicate matters, as societies with more positive views on sexuality may be less inclined to label certain behaviors as addiction.

> Societies with more positive views on sexuality may be
> less inclined to label certain behaviors as addiction.

Many sex addicts feel guilt, shame, or remorse, yet appear unable to control their actions. They often experience hopelessness and helplessness, rooted in their inability to establish intimacy. These feelings can lead to depression, loneliness, fear, anxiety, and even suicidal thoughts. The case of Leonardo shows that the condition may stem from a combination of biological, psychological, and societal factors.

THEORETICAL PERSPECTIVES

Some of the theories as to why sex addiction occurs are neurophysiological, whereas others tend to be more developmental.[7] From a neurological standpoint, some argue that abnormalities in the temporal lobes contribute to sexual addiction, while frontal lobe damage may lead to disinhibited behaviors, increasing sexual activity and reducing self-control. It is also hypothesized that sexual disinhibition may be the result of imbalances in some neurotransmitters, such as the highly addictive dopamine. Further investigation, however, is needed to clarify these neurological irregularities.

Other theories suggest that sexual addiction emerges as both a consequence of and coping mechanism for early childhood trauma, including sexual abuse. Dysfunctional family dynamics during childhood may have left the needs of these individuals unmet, leading to a persistent sense of loss. As a result, some—like Leonardo—act out sexually because they never learned healthier ways to experience intimacy.

> Some sex addicts act out sexually because they
> never learned healthier ways to experience intimacy.

Many sex addicts seem to have a history of childhood physical or sexual abuse. For these individuals, compulsive sexual activities become a source of emotional relief. They use sex as a form of escape from emotional and psychological problems such as stress, anxiety, depression, and social isolation.

In addition, individuals who grew up in households where one or both parents displayed addictive behaviors are significantly more likely to develop a sex addiction.[8] Given its seemingly uncontrollable nature, sex addiction often co-occurs with impulse control disorder, obsessive-compulsive disorder, relationship issues, and substance use disorders.[9]

SEX ADDICTION TREATMENT

People like Leonardo are unlikely to ask for help: a common issue among sex addicts due to the social stigma attached to their behavior. Many are overwhelmed by shame and guilt. Media stigmatization and the criminalization of sexual offenses have also created an environment that discourages treatment and prevention. No wonder that many sex addicts feel trapped. This is often worsened by co-occurring personality disorders, including substance abuse, which many use to lower inhibitions, cope with shame and guilt, or alleviate depression. With so many factors at play, it's no surprise that many are reluctant to seek help.

What many sex addicts may not realize is that there *are* effective intervention techniques available to help them overcome their addiction.[10] Naturally, the first step is to recognize the problem. To break the cycle of obsessive thoughts and behaviors, they must be willing to ask for help. However, sex addicts often ignore the darker side of their addiction. As seen in the case of Leonardo, they jeopardize their relationships, careers, finances, health, and the well-being of their partners. Ultimately, they face a choice: confront and eliminate the addiction, or risk being consumed by it.

> Ultimately, sex addicts face a choice: confront and eliminate the addiction, or risk being consumed by it.

As far as treatments are concerned, there are several possible routes:

- *Psychopharmacological assistance.* Certain antidepressants and hormonal medications can help reduce sexual drive by targeting brain chemicals linked to obsessive thoughts and behaviors. These drugs diminish the "rewards" that compulsive sexual behaviors provide, thereby lowering sexual urges. However, rarely does medication eradicate or resolve compulsive sexuality in the long term.
- *One-on-one cognitive or psychodynamic therapy.* This seems to be a more effective way of dealing with sexual addiction. These treatments can help reframe experiences and address unresolved trauma or emotional pain. By identifying the thought patterns and false beliefs that contribute to addictive behaviors, individuals can gain insight into the roots of their actions. Trauma-informed therapy, in particular, may help people process traumatic childhood experiences and develop healthier ways of coping. It can be a highly effective way of assisting them in overcoming their sense of loss.

> By identifying the thought patterns and false beliefs
> that contribute to addictive behaviors, individuals
> can gain insight into the roots of their actions.

- *Group-oriented interventions.* Inpatient treatment centers provide sex addiction recovery programs that typically include in-depth individual and group therapy sessions. By stepping away from their usual environments, addicts can focus on regaining control of their impulses and begin the healing process. One of the advantages of group-based interventions is that people feel less isolated. Realizing that others also suffer from this addiction can help alleviate the shame and guilt often associated with it.
- *12-step programs.* These are similar to the model used by Alcoholics Anonymous, such as Sex Addicts Anonymous (SAA). SAA provides a self-help recovery framework and support group that can be highly effective for people struggling with compulsive sexual behavior and its related issues. A key benefit of these groups is the support network they offer, fostering a sense of accountability among participants. It is important to note, however, that participants in these programs aren't required to give up sex entirely but are encouraged to refrain from compulsive and destructive sexual behavior.
- *Couple or family counseling.* This may be an appropriate treatment option. This type of therapy can help restore trust, reduce shame and guilt, and foster a healthier sexual relationship between partners.

As seen in Leonardo's case, sex addicts face a unique set of challenges. But as is the case for other addictions, overcoming compulsion is not easy but very much worth the effort. Given the many negative consequences of addictive behavior, taking action leads to a more fulfilling life. However, addressing addiction requires time, sacrifice, and willpower, and there is always the risk of relapse.

> As is the case for other addictions, overcoming
> compulsion is not easy but very much worth the effort.

HOMO SAPIENS OR HOMO SEXUALIS

Sex and reproduction are part of life. Like other animals, humans are biologically programmed to eat, sleep, reproduce, and raise offspring. Although sex is a primary instinct driven by genetics to ensure reproduction, for humans it goes beyond procreation as it has the potential to be a very pleasurable activity.

In this respect, human beings seem to have transcended their evolutionary destiny. Unlike other mammals, whose behavior is primarily guided by instinct, *Homo sapiens* is endowed with reason and humans can make independent decisions concerning their own behavior. *Homo sapiens* is more inclined to have sex purely for pleasure.

As a result of this added dimension, sex can also be a means of enriching connections between people. It is one of the great equalizers in human life: whether rich or poor, smart or stupid, good-looking or ugly, everyone can experience orgasmic pleasure. In this respect, sex is an equal opportunity provider. For many people, a loving sexual connection is the closest experience to a transcendent sense of benevolence, bliss, and the feeling that all is well. Therefore, a satisfactory sex life should be seen as a great form of self-care, acting as a socially beneficial, powerful bond between people. However, for sex addicts, this potential is distorted, turning sex into a destructive force. Hence, they must take steps to deal more constructively with their feelings of loss.

For many people, a loving sexual connection is the closest experience to a transcendent sense of benevolence, bliss, and the feeling that all is well.

Whether as a force for good or bad, sexuality greatly influences the world we live in. As the American novelist Henry Miller once said, "What holds the world together, as I have learned from bitter experience, is sexual intercourse."[11] Indeed, sex is so vital that it underpins politics, economics, and the overall psychological well-being of a society. Sexuality can elevate and connect people. It provides a social structure, and this is where morality enters the picture, particularly sexual morality. Here, "morality" refers to adherence—or lack thereof—to a set of behavioral standards or norms. This notion of morality also introduces the concept of sin, where failure to meet these moral standards leads to immoral acts or human transgressions.

Sex is so vital that it underpins politics, economics, and the overall psychological well-being of a society.

While animals know no sin, for humans, sexuality is often intertwined with sin and morality. For this reason, sexuality has been subjected to many rules delineating what is considered morally acceptable sexual behavior. This has led to the rise of moral guardians who determine what is and isn't permitted, as well as systems to "police" this behavior. However, there is often a gap between these restrictive societal pronouncements and the reality of sexual practices. This creates an ongoing balancing act, with conservative views focusing on procreation and libertarian perspectives emphasizing pleasure. This indicates the controversial nature of sexuality.

> While animals know no sin, for humans, sexuality is often intertwined with sin and morality.

Given the power wielded by moral guardians over sexuality, avoidance often becomes the name of the game, and sexual matters are frequently swept under the rug. We see, but we don't want to see. This conscious and unconscious blindness makes personal sex lives a taboo topic in everyday conversation, despite the extent to which sexuality permeates public life. While sexuality takes up a considerable amount of space in people's minds, many remain fairly squeamish and uncomfortable with the instinctual aspects of human behavior. In fact, what should be a natural topic is often perceived as dirty—people rarely discuss what they did in bed the night before. Thus, although sex is ubiquitous, it is rarely talked about openly, particularly in relation to its impact on mental health. Sexual addiction is even more taboo, often shrouded in a conspiracy of silence. Many deny its existence, but as we've seen with cases like Leonardo's, such behavior can cause great harm and pain both to the individuals involved and those around them.

> There is often a gap between restrictive societal pronouncements and the reality of sexual practices. This creates an ongoing balancing act, with conservative views focusing on procreation and libertarian perspectives emphasizing pleasure.

Despite the discomfort surrounding discussions of sexual addiction, it is a subject that must be addressed. While the guardians of public morality may fear the transgressive nature of sexual disorders, ignoring the issue doesn't make it go away. As a relatively common disorder with significant personal and public health ramifications, it is time to bring sexual addiction out of the shadows. While sex can be fun, playful, and meaningful, being obsessed with it spells trouble. Leonardo's case warns us that sexual desires should not become self-destructive or an all-consuming force. As the English writer G.K. Chesterton said so succinctly, "The moment sex ceases to be a servant, it becomes a tyrant."[12]

Conscious and unconscious blindness makes personal
sex lives a taboo topic in everyday conversation, despite
the extent to which sexuality permeates public life.

As sex addicts squander their life, do they even realize their loss? Or perhaps they agree with the Roman moralist Publilius Syrus, who wrote, "The loss that is not known is no loss."[13]

While the guardians of public morality may fear
the transgressive nature of sexual disorders,
ignoring the issue doesn't make it go away.

NOTES

1 D. H. Lawrence (1928). *Lady Chatterley's Lover.* New York: Nelson Doubleday, Chapter VI.

2 John Bowlby (1969). *Attachment. Attachment and Loss: Vol. 1. Loss.* New York: Basic Books.

3 American Psychiatric Association (2022). *Diagnostic and Statistical Manual of Mental Disorders, Fifth Edition (DSM-5-TR).* Washington, DC: APA.

4 World Health Organization (2025). Sexual health: Overview. www.who.int/health-topics/sexual-health#tab=tab_1

5 Laurent Karila, Aline Wéry, Aviv Weinstein, Olivier Cottencin, Aymeric Petit, Michel Reynaud, and Joel Billieux (2014). Sexual addiction or hypersexual disorder: Different terms for the same problem? A review of the literature. *Current Pharmaceutical Design,* 20(25), 4012–4020; B. R. Sahithya and Rithvik Kasyap (2022). Sexual Addiction Disorder—a review with recent updates. *Journal of Psychosocial Health,* 4(2), 95–101. https://medium.com/@infinitepassion/sex-addiction-80-are-men-4fe2b5874df7

6 Timothy Fong (2006). Understanding and managing compulsive sexual behaviors. *Psychiatry,* 3(11), 51–58.

7 George Koob and Nora Volkow (2016). Neurobiology of addiction: A neurocircuitry analysis. *Lancet Psychiatry,* 3(8), 760–773; Katherine Derbyshire and Jon E. Grant (2015). Compulsive sexual behavior: A review of the literature. *Journal of Behavioral Addictions,* 4(2), 37–43; Shane W. Kraus, Valerie Voon, and Marc N. Potenza (2016). Neurobiology of compulsive sexual behavior: Emerging science. *Neuropsychopharmacology,* 41(1), 385–386; Mayo Foundation for Medical Education and Research (2023, April 19). *Compulsive Sexual Behavior.* Mayo Clinic. www.mayoclinic.org/diseases-conditions/compulsive-sexual-behavior/symptoms-causes/syc-20360434

8 Kenneth S. Kendler, Carol A. Prescott, John Myers, and Michael C. Neale (2003). The structure of genetic and environmental risk factors for common psychiatric and substance use disorders in men and women. *Archives of General Psychiatry,* 60(9), 929–937.

9 Vincent Estellon and Harold Mouras (2012). Sexual addiction: Insights from psychoanalysis and functional neuroimaging. *Socioaffective Neuroscience & Psychology,* 2, 11814. https://doi.org/10.3402/snp.v2io.11814

10 Eli Coleman, Nancy Raymond, and Anne McBean (2003). Assessment and treatment of compulsive sexual behavior. *Minnesota Medicine Magazine,* 86, 42–47.

11 Henry Miller (2015/1939). *Tropic of Capricorn.* Harmondsworth, UK: Penguin.

12 G. K. Chesterton (1923). *St Francis of Assisi.* London: Hodder and Stoughton.

13 Publilius Syrus Sententiae (1934/1st century BC). *Minor Latin Poets, Volume I: Publilius Syrus. Elegies on Maecenas. Grattius. Calpurnius Siculus. Laus Pisonis. Einsiedeln Eclogues. Aetna.* Loeb Classical Library 284. Trans. J. Wight and A. M. Duff. Cambridge, MA: Harvard University Press, pp. 36–37.

12

WHAT IS YOUR BODY TELLING YOU?

If a man thinks about his physical or moral condition, he generally finds that he is ill.
—Johann Wolfgang von Goethe[1]

The human body is the best picture of the human soul.
—Ludwig Wittgenstein[2]

The loss some people experience in the realm of sexuality can be understood more broadly. Just as sexual addicts suffer, others may also become disconnected from their bodies, feeling a sense of detachment. This can be seen as another type of loss—losing control over one's physical self. A darkly humorous example illustrates this idea.

During lunch at the office cafeteria, a group of executives sat around casually chatting. The conversation took a more serious turn as they began to complain about what was wrong with their bodies. They had all experienced some form of loss.

> "Sadly enough, my legs aren't as strong as they used to be," one of them said. "I used to bike to work, and I really enjoyed it. Now, it tires me out, and I have to take the subway instead. Sometimes, given my physical condition, I wonder if something more serious is going on."
>
> "I know what you mean!" another replied. "This past year, my eyesight has really gone downhill. It's been so stressful watching it deteriorate. I can barely read the signs at the end of the cafeteria anymore. Sometimes, I worry I might be going blind."
>
> "Recently, I've been finding it very hard to turn my head. It hurts so much," said a third. "I can't help but wonder if I have a serious case of arthritis or some kind of deadly muscular disease. These pains are getting me down."

DOI: 10.4324/9781003651260-14

"Listening to all of you, it sounds like we're all going downhill," another chimed in. "In my case, ever since I started taking medication for high blood pressure, I've been having dizzy spells. Now, I'm starting to wonder if there's something more serious going on. Sometimes, I even think I might have cancer."

"Clearly, aging is not for sissies. I guess that's the price we pay for getting older," another member of the group remarked.

They all became quiet for a while. Then, one executive broke the silence with a touch of humor, "Well, at least I can still walk!"

Tragicomical as this interaction may seem, we often hear similar conversations filled with exaggerated concerns about physical health. Beyond the natural process of aging, the lingering effects of the Covid-19 pandemic continue to impact people both physically and mentally. Stress-related disorders have surged, contributing to reduced employee engagement, increased mental health-related absenteeism, and higher staff turnover. In addition, mental health issues have brought about a rise in somatic complaints—an indicator of people's state of mind.[3] It begs the question, "What have we truly lost?"

SOMATIC SYMPTOM DISORDER (SSD)

Of course, somatic complaints are nothing new. They've always been part of the human condition. For some, these complaints are central to their lives. In fact, the *Diagnostic and Statistical Manual of Mental Disorders (DSM-V)*[4] includes a diagnosis called somatic symptom disorder (SSD), a condition that used to be called hypochondria. People with SSD have excessive and unrealistic worries about their health. They tend to misinterpret minor symptoms as signs of a serious disease. They feel at a loss regarding what is happening to their body. For example, a person with a headache might be convinced they have a brain tumor. Or someone with an upset stomach might fear they have stomach cancer. Despite the lack of a medical diagnosis, they persist in believing they have a serious physical disorder and will go to great lengths to find a physiological explanation. At the same time, the discomfort they feel is very real, deepening their sense of confusion and loss.

Not surprisingly, given their preoccupations, people with SSD often engage in repeated health check-ups. Even when doctors rule out any serious illness, their concerns do not alleviate. Instead of accepting the medical evaluation, they challenge it or insist that the doctor has made a mistake. Some even go as far as to seek out a doctor who will agree that they have a serious illness. The obsessiveness associated with SSD is not under their voluntary control.

These individuals often desperately seek a specific diagnosis, believing that naming their condition will solve their problem. Although naming a disorder may offer some relief, it's merely a step toward addressing it. The real challenge lies in managing and treating the condition. However, not all diagnosed conditions can be easily fixed. Many sufferers of chronic or complex conditions are frustrated when there is no quick fix.

> Individuals with somatic symptom disorder often desperately seek a specific diagnosis, believing that naming their condition will solve their problem.

People suffering from SSD often focus so much on their health concerns that they can no longer function adequately. Their mood stays negative, marked by feelings of anger, depression, fatigue, and anxiety, which can strain their relationships. After all, no one likes to hang around people who constantly whine and moan about their health. Working with chronic complainers can be annoying and exhausting.

> Working with chronic complainers can be annoying and exhausting.

IDENTIFYING SSD

Diagnosing SSD can be quite difficult, as people with this disorder are convinced that their symptoms and distress are physical, not psychological. However, several features characterize SSD:

- One or more physical symptoms that are distressing or disrupt daily life.
- Concerns about health that are disproportionate to the seriousness of the symptoms.
- Symptoms unrelated to any identifiable medical cause.
- Belief that normal physical sensations are signs of illness.
- Excessive time and energy spent on symptoms or health concerns, often feeling that medical professionals haven't provided a thorough examination or treatment.
- At least one persistent symptom, though the specific symptoms may come and go over time.

THE ORIGINS OF SSD

SSD can develop at any point in life, but it most often begins in early adulthood. It can affect both men and women, although women are far more likely to report somatic symptoms. One possible explanation for this difference is the link between SSD and childhood abuse or trauma, to which women are more frequently exposed.[5]

Although the exact cause of SSD isn't clear, various factors likely contribute, including genetic and biological ones. For instance, some individuals may have a lower pain threshold. Beyond "nature," "nurture" also plays a significant part, especially through family dynamics. Exaggerated somatic concerns may stem from a learned behavior. Children, for example, may mirror a parent who's always overly concerned about disease or overreacts to minor illnesses. Family dynamics may also result in people developing problems in processing emotions. Instead of addressing their emotional issues, they may prefer to use physical symptoms to get attention. In addition, many people with SSD have experienced loss or stressful events, such as the recent Covid-19 pandemic, which can put somatic concerns into overdrive.

> Instead of addressing their emotional issues, they may prefer to use physical symptoms to get attention.

LIVING WITH SSD

How to address SSD? The first step is a thorough medical examination to rule out any physical causes for the symptoms. If none is found, medical practitioners may refer the person to a psychiatrist, psychologist, or other health care professional, especially if SSD is suspected. The psychiatrist or psychologist can then make a diagnosis based on the person's attitudes and behaviors.

During this process, it's important to remember that even though there is no medical cause for the symptoms, the problem is still very real and serious. The person is genuinely suffering and experiencing a sense of loss. Therefore, healthcare professionals shouldn't downplay the concerns of the patient. They should realize that living with SSD can be extremely difficult.

> It's important to remember that even though there is no medical cause for the symptoms, the problem is still very real and serious. The person is genuinely suffering and experiencing a sense of loss.

The challenge for health practitioners is that most people with SSD refuse to believe that their symptoms stem from mental or emotional distress. For this reason, they tend to resist psychotherapeutic interventions. Consequently, only a small percentage of people with SSD fully recover.

Still, individuals suffering from SSD would do well to get treatment to prevent their symptoms from worsening, as the disorder impairs their quality of life. They must learn to manage and control these symptoms, as well as minimize the interpersonal problems associated with them. Providing an understanding and supportive environment can help decrease the severity of symptoms and help the person cope better.

Dynamic psychotherapy can be a good starting point for treating SSD. It explores the origins of the problem to motivate the person to experiment with healthier ways of living. If a person with SSD also has a mood or anxiety disorder, combining dynamic psychotherapy with antidepressants or anti-anxiety drugs can be very effective. Furthermore, cognitive therapy (a type of psychotherapy that helps individuals change their patterns of thinking) is valuable for addressing the thoughts and emotions that fuel the symptoms. It can help the person find better ways to manage stress and function in social and work environments.

Mindfulness therapy, when combined with cognitive therapy, can further enhance awareness of thoughts, feelings, and actions that hinder progress. Regular practice of stress management and relaxation techniques can also help individuals clear their minds of negative thoughts that contribute to health anxiety.

With perseverance, those suffering from somatic symptom disorder (SSD) can change the story their body is telling them and regain the quality of life they've lost. It is a feeling of loss that can be managed.

All in all, it is advisable for people suffering from SSD to learn how to manage stress, find ways to cope with their physical symptoms, and reduce their mental preoccupation with these concerns. However, they should not expect things to change overnight. Persistence is key. With proper therapy and counseling, they can begin the journey toward a better quality of life. Importantly, the sense of loss they feel about their life doesn't need to be permanent. With perseverance, they can change the story their body is telling them and regain the quality of life they've lost. It is a feeling of loss that can be managed.

NOTES

1 Johann Wolfgang von Goethe (1906/c. 1809–1836). Life and character. In *The Maxims and Reflections of Goethe*. Trans. Bailey Saunders. New York: The Macmillan Company, Section II, reflection 75.

2 Author's translation of the original: *Der menschliche Körper ist das beste Bild der menschlichen Seele.* Ludwig Wittgenstein (1953). *Philosophische Untersuchungen.* London: Blackwell, published posthumously.

3 World Health Organization (2022, March 22). COVID-19 pandemic triggers 25% increase in prevalence of anxiety and depression worldwide: Wake-up call to all countries to step up mental health services and support. www.who.int/news/item/02-03-2022-covid-19-pandemic-triggers-25-increase-in-prevalence-of-anxiety-and-depression-worldwide

4 American Psychiatric Association (2013). *Diagnostic and Statistical Manual of Mental Disorders (DSM-5).* Washington, DC: American Psychiatric Publishing.

5 World Health Organization (2021, March 9). *Violence Against Women Prevalence Estimates, 2018.* www.who.int/publications/i/item/9789240022256

13

BEING AND NOTHINGNESS

Life is not a problem to be solved, but a reality to be experienced.

—Jacobus Johannes Leeuw[1]

Those who make the worst use of their time are the first to complain of its brevity.

—Jean de la Bruyère[2]

As described in previous chapters, people cope with loss, in all its myriad forms inherent to the human condition, in different ways. Some individuals fight against it, doing everything possible to deny its reality. They skillfully use defense mechanisms and may be masters of repression. Others don't possess this talent. They may give up or become depressed. They may lose themselves in grief or anger. For some, work becomes their way of dealing with existential concerns—particularly anxiety about life's transience. "Manic" work habits serve as a distraction, a way to avoid facing the painful truths of their condition. The inevitability of death being too overwhelming, some bury themselves in work to keep it at bay.

The inevitability of death being too overwhelming, some individuals bury themselves in work to keep it at bay.

Yet, what they are trying to accomplish remains vague, and this also holds true for their mission in life. However, beneath their relentless busyness, we can discern the presence of death—the stealth motivator—driving their actions from the shadows.

DOI: 10.4324/9781003651260-15

> Beneath a workaholic's relentless busyness, we can discern the presence of death—the stealth motivator—driving their actions from the shadows.

THE MANIC DEFENSE

The knowledge of our inevitable death presents a conundrum for many. Some are so afraid of death that they never truly live. It is as if they tiptoe through life, in an attempt to arrive safely at death. They don't pay heed to Socrates' admonition that "the unexamined life is not worth living."[3] Constantly worrying about dying robs them of the joy of living.

> Some individuals are so afraid of death that they never truly live. It is as if they tiptoe through life, in an attempt to arrive safely at death.

Instead, they bury their death anxiety deep in their unconscious, going through life in a robotic manner, as if expecting to carry on indefinitely. To distract themselves, they resort to "manic" distractions—mindless, often trivial activities that provide a false sense of accomplishment. Rather than seizing life, they are "killing time" with unimportant tasks. Sadly, they aren't aware that time is killing them.

> Rather than seizing life, some people are "killing time" with unimportant tasks. Sadly, they aren't aware that time is killing them.

In that sense, it could be argued that their lives end long before their actual death. Living a life that has very little meaning, they clearly have a hard time accepting that life is temporary. They don't realize that death itself is not the greatest loss. The greatest loss is what dies inside them while they're still alive. They fail to see that the meaning of life is not something to be discovered after death in some hidden, mysterious realm. Rather, it can be found here and now, by living as fully and creatively as possible.

> Certain individuals don't realize that death itself is not the greatest loss. The greatest loss is what dies inside them while they're still alive.

What these individuals should understand is that the awareness of death could give them more of a stake in life. Accepting mortality can serve as a clarion call to live to the fullest, to enjoy every moment of the life they've been given. Instead of falling into the abyss of hopelessness, they should see death as a reason to embrace life.

Accepting mortality can serve as a clarion call to live to the fullest.

For some, the fear of death may stem from a fear of life itself. The concept of self-reflection—exploring what gives life meaning—may seem quite strange to them. Preoccupied with what's to come, they don't question why they live as they do. They're reluctant to ask themselves meaningful questions. As a result, they feel disconnected from their emotional life, hopes, fears, and desires.

Workaholics should wonder why they're working themselves to death. What makes them so obsessed with work? What's driving them? What fantasies hitch themselves to their constant busyness? Only by stepping away from their frenzied activities can they obtain a modicum of insight into their behavior. Taking this journey, however, can be quite scary. They may fear what they will uncover. Workaholism helps them push away the demons that haunt them.

However we look at it, "workaholism" remains a highly dysfunctional way of coping with anxiety about death. It is an ineffective way of dealing with the underlying sense of loss. In this context, workaholics are losing out in a big way—they're losing out on life. Instead of leading a fulfilling existence, they use incessant activity to keep depressive thoughts at bay.

Workaholics should wonder why they're working themselves to death.

These individuals often rush from one task to the next, unable to tolerate even brief periods of inactivity. For them, even leisure time consists of "shoulds" and "have tos" that must be checked off a physical or mental to-do list. Driven by their fear of confronting death anxiety head-on, they are unable to control their frantic work habits. To them, life seems unimaginable without the constant distraction of work. In this way, work wards off depressive thoughts, props up a fragile sense of self-esteem, and becomes a means of self-affirmation. In other words, workaholics try to find meaning in the structure and pace of their work life, and if that disappears, they lose their purpose and direction.

Workaholics try to find meaning in the structure and pace of their work life, and if that disappears, they lose their purpose and direction.

Unfortunately, for workaholics, no amount of activity will ever be enough. Complicating matters, in today's organizations these individuals are highly encouraged, supported, and rewarded for their unhealthy behavior patterns. Moreover, the development of workaholism may be difficult to counter because many organizations value such behavior for its perceived contribution to the bottom line. Yet, the leaders of these organizations don't realize that fostering a workaholic culture can lead to serious problems. These range from low morale, depression, substance abuse, and workplace harassment, to personal issues such as divorce and above-average absenteeism, all of which can result in chaos in the workplace.

The development of workaholism may be difficult to counter because many organizations value such behavior for its perceived contribution to the bottom line.

As noted earlier, these workaholic behavior patterns can be labeled as a "manic defense"—a way to distract the conscious mind from feelings of helplessness and despair. It manifests as a flurry of activity that generates temporary feelings of euphoria, purpose, and an illusion of control. However, this avoidance of reality is only effective for a limited time. As the saying goes, what we push out through the door may come back in through the window. Despite their efforts, death anxiety will not go away, and feelings of distress may even intensify. Of course, it's worth noting that we all use manic defenses to some extent, but workaholics take it several steps too far.

As the saying goes, what we push out through the door may come back in through the window.

REAL WORK

How we psychologically process our anxiety about death—the ultimate form of loss—determines whether we find work meaningful or meaningless. As American president Franklin D. Roosevelt said:

> Happiness lies not in the mere possession of money; it lies in the joy of achievement, in the thrill of creative effort. The joy and moral stimulation of work no longer must be forgotten in the mad chase of evanescent profits. These dark days will be worth all they cost us if they teach us that our true destiny is not to be ministered unto but to minister to ourselves and to our fellow men.[4]

But, as I have been trying to convey, there is a difference between "manic" work activities and truly meaningful, real work. Innovative work, or any creation that deviates from routine tasks and is valued by the creator, spectator, or consumer as something special, is the kind of activity that holds meaning. When that's the case, our drive to defeat death is sustained by the hope and belief that what we are creating has lasting worth and will outlive death and decay.

> Innovative work, or any creation that deviates from routine tasks and is valued by the creator, spectator, or consumer as something special, is the kind of activity that holds meaning.

Of course, living in alignment with this belief is easier said than done. People often ignore Plato's insightful words:

> For to fear death, gentlemen, is nothing else than to think one is wise when one is not; for it is thinking one knows what one does not know. For no one knows whether death be not even the greatest of all blessings to man, but they fear it as if they knew that it is the greatest of evils.[5]

By examining workaholism, I aim to highlight that death may not be the greatest loss we experience in life. As mentioned before, the greatest loss may be what dies inside us while we are still alive.

> Death may not be the greatest loss we experience in life; the greatest loss may be what dies inside us while we are still alive.

A CASE EXPLORATION

Consider the story of Alexander. As he worked increasingly long hours to get his financial startup off the ground, Alexander's satisfaction with his life had reached rock bottom. He found himself questioning the fundamentals of his existence. His low mood reflected the turmoil of his mind. He was grappling with unsettling questions: What was he doing with his life? Did it have any purpose or meaning? Was there anything to look forward to?

These questions stemmed from a deep sense of loneliness and isolation. Although his company was growing rapidly, Alexander didn't feel connected to his co-founders and colleagues. His involvement gave him very little satisfaction. His home life was also nothing to brag about. He and his wife were like ships passing in the night, living more like distant roommates than partners. In fact, their sex life was non-existent.

To make matters worse, Alexander had also neglected his health and become overweight. As he took stock of his life, he realized that the very foundations of his existence were shaken. He knew that he had depressive tendencies, but what he was now experiencing went far beyond anything he had felt before. He began to wonder whether he was in the midst of some existential crisis—whatever that meant.

What was happening to Alexander? Was his present hyperactivity at work just a way to push aside how he really felt? Without the structure of work, would he become even more depressed? Alexander no longer knew what was truly important—what was it that he was living for? He recognized how difficult it was to confront his own mortality. How was he supposed to face life's fundamental nothingness?

Alexander felt as though a tape was playing through his mind, repeating questions like: "What's the purpose of my life? Is it all work until I drop dead? Does anything I do really matter? Does anyone actually care about me? Is there even such a thing as living happily ever after?"

For as long as Alexander could remember, finding purpose in his work had been crucial to him. It had always helped him function at his best. But now, that sense of purpose had completely evaporated. If he was truly honest with himself, he had reached a dead end. He even had suicidal thoughts. Despite never having been a religious person, he had begun to envy those with faith. At least, their belief in an afterlife brought them a degree of comfort.

Alexander then became plagued by terrifying dreams. In one recurrent dream, he found himself walking through a swampy area, only to be swallowed by a black hole. Waking up in a sweat, he would reassure himself that dreams have no meaning.

But was that truly the case? Was he deluding himself? In reality, Alexander saw that repressing uncomfortable thoughts had always been one of his stronger defenses. Yet, this way of dealing with life appeared to be no longer working. Perhaps these nightmares were a warning sign. No matter how much he tried to push the dark thoughts away, they felt all too real. He vividly recalled his last nightmare—how terrifying it was to wake up to his heart pounding, his chest hurting, and struggling to breathe.

Perhaps the greatest tragedy is a life that ends too early on the despairing side of the abyss, where meaning has collapsed.

Were these panic attacks connected to his outlook on life? To his sense of losing control? To his loneliness? These gloomy thoughts reminded him of a quote by the French philosopher Jean-Paul Sartre: "Human life begins on the far side of despair."[6] Perhaps the greatest tragedy is a life that ends too early on the despairing side of the abyss, where meaning has collapsed.

Whatever the case, Alexander felt drained, useless, and ineffective. Life had once seemed so much simpler. Now, he had no one to turn to—no one he could talk to about his angst. His wife was too busy with her career. He was an only child whose parents had passed away. His workaholism had led him to neglect the few friends he had made; besides, they were all in different time zones. Now he was at a loss for what to do next.

The crumbling of defenses

Of course, it's easy to suggest that Alexander's dissatisfaction with his work and his perfunctory marriage was the cause of his malaise. And true enough, two of the major reasons for living had shaky foundations. But perhaps there was more at play, and his struggles were mere catalysts. Most likely, Alexander was going through an existential crisis—a fundamental struggle to accept the finite nature of our existence. Anxiety about death can cause significant discomfort, whether conscious or unconscious, manifesting in various affective, cognitive, developmental, and socio-cultural reactions.

When unresolved, death anxiety can result in heightened stress and even psychological burnout. No wonder that, throughout history, human societies have developed structures, symbols, narratives, and rituals to deal with it. In fact, motivation is largely derived from our death anxiety.

Throughout history, human societies have developed structures, symbols, narratives, and rituals to deal with death anxiety.

The good news is that death anxiety can be properly harnessed. It needn't result in loss. It has motivated countless people to engage in creative, meaningful activities. And when I refer to creative work, I'm not just speaking of artists, writers, musicians, or scientists.

Others look at transcending death by leaving behind a legacy, something that will serve as a reminder of their existence. For example, Alfred Lord Tennyson, the famous poet, said, "So many worlds, so much to do, So little done, such things to be."[7] His comment reflects the sentiment shared by many creative people that they don't have enough time to finish their life's work. Their fear of death often stems from the worry that they won't fulfill their mission in life. This great urge to leave a legacy drives them. Ultimately, to be prepared for death, we must first be prepared to live well. The ability to die well comes from having lived well.

The ability to die well comes from having lived well.

Once more, it raises the question of whether we have given sufficient thought to the role of meaning in our lives.[8] It could very well be that meaning has fallen by the wayside as we've focused on the business of making a living. However, with our impending death, we may find ourselves turning more toward the search for meaning. Often unnoticed, this search can serve as a psychological defense against the fear of death. In fact, meaning management motivates us to embrace life and to engage fully in living, regardless of our physical condition or circumstances.

Meaning management is not just rationalization or cognitive reframing; it involves the reconstruction and transformation of our values, beliefs, and meaning systems. The best way to prepare for death is to live life to the fullest. As Marcus Aurelius wisely said, "No one ever escapes the day of his fate: his thought should be on . . . how best to live his life in the time he has to be alive."[9]

When reflecting on the inevitability of death, we must also be willing to let go and detach ourselves from events and things that we used to value. A helpful exercise in this process could be a life review. This offers an opportunity to revisit and evaluate our life experiences, to help us identify our current goals and fine-tune our focus on what truly matters at this stage of life. Such an exercise can bring order and coherence to our life. It may lead to self-acceptance and a deeper understanding of what we have stood for before we die.

When reflecting on the inevitability of death, we must also be willing to let go and detach ourselves from events and things that we used to value.

It is important that we embrace the life we have lived. We must connect with the inner essence of our being. As one of the characters in Haruki Murakami's short story *Landscape with Flatiron* says: "I've never once thought about how I was going to die . . . I can't think about it. I don't even know how I'm going to live."[10]

However, Alexander's initial response to his existential crisis—a common response, in fact—was to immerse himself in "busyness." It became his habitual defense. Pushing away thoughts of death by fleeing into action can be tempting. By resorting to this "manic defense" and engaging in a frenzy of activities, Alexander clung to an unrealistic belief in his ability to deal with the vicissitudes of life. This was his way of searching for purpose. But as Alexander found out the hard way, that defense wasn't foolproof. Eventually, it stopped being effective.

Pushing away thoughts of death by fleeing into action can be tempting.

We can hypothesize that his dissatisfaction with work and the impasse in his marriage brought matters to a head. These factors built toward a tipping point, pushing him to question his role in the larger scheme of things. It forced him to confront questions about his existence: What is my greater purpose? How should I live my life?

Questions like these forced Alexander to face life's temporary nature and contributed to his deep sense of isolation—his lack of a community. They made him realize that, despite all his defensive maneuvers, the meaning of life is intertwined with death; that life and death are bound together in intricate ways, with death as an immovable presence. The shadow of mortality was hard to push away, and Alexander had been receiving many reminders. Even with his formidable arsenal of defenses, the looming presence of existential anxiety and depression was very real.

This doesn't mean that all is lost. For Alexander, as for all of us, despite their emotional toll, these concerns can also lead to a heightened awareness of life. An existential crisis can be viewed as a blessing in disguise. It can propel us into action. Death anxiety may motivate us to search for what truly gives our lives meaning and rethink what we've been doing.

Death anxiety may motivate us to search for what truly gives
our lives meaning and rethink what we've been doing.

Feeling real

This experience of nothingness forced Alexander to question his present way of living. The challenge was to move from nothingness to "somethingness"—that is, purpose. His anxiety about the finiteness of life became the starting point for a deeper search for authenticity, community, and meaning. It encouraged him to question things he had not previously dared to question and to reflect on what he had long suppressed. Gradually, his existential crisis led to greater self-awareness and self-knowledge. It marked the beginning of a journey to uncover his life's real purpose.

Ultimately, his existential malaise enabled him to take responsibility for his life and take meaningful action.

The tipping point came when Alexander decided to take time off and spend a weekend with his best friend. Their long conversations helped him break free from his self-imposed prison and reframe his life situation. Stepping away from his daily busyness helped him put his challenges into perspective.

Alexander concluded that dwelling on the misery of the human condition wasn't constructive, nor was fixating on his fear of nonexistence. He realized that although we can never escape the reality of death, we can transform death anxiety through our capacity for building meaning and connection. Through building, loving, and creating, we can turn life into a personal adventure.

> Although we can never escape the reality of death,
> we can transform death anxiety through our
> capacity for building meaning and connection.

It became clear to Alexander that meaning in life wouldn't simply come to him; he was responsible for creating it. He was responsible for building a sense of community and belonging. It was up to him to pull himself out of his malaise. He had to take an honest look at himself—facing both the pains and the pleasures. He had to work through his depression, anxieties, loneliness, and sense of loss. He needed to accept who he truly was. Only by doing this could he figure out how to be happy.

For too long, Alexander had ignored what was actually happening in his life. He had tried to ignore that he didn't really enjoy his work and that his marriage had been languishing. Despite his successes at work and the fact that his marriage had once been a great adventure, the past was the past. The present was starkly different. His previous professional achievements had not dissolved his feelings of emptiness, nor had they provided him with true satisfaction. It was as if he had been using fig leaves to cover an emotional void. His inability to have a frank dialogue with himself had only deepened his concerns about authenticity, meaning, and community. What had once been lingering doubts had now reached a breaking point.

> It was as if he had been using fig leaves to cover an emotional void.

Although Alexander came to accept that we are essentially alone in the world, he still longed for connection. He yearned to find a place he could call home—a supportive community where he could make a difference. He realized that a sense of belonging and meaning could serve as powerful anti-dotes to the existential anxiety that had been weighing him down.

Alexander's existential angst helped him become more open to life's reali-ties; it forced him to stop lying to himself. He came to see that his existential crisis had a positive side. It pushed him out of his comfort zone and helped him reframe his situation. He realized that people have free will and can be participants, not just observers, in their own lives. But it was up to him to give his life purpose, value, and meaning. If he wanted his life to be meaningful, he needed to take greater personal responsibility for his future. If he wanted to live fully, he couldn't let life drift by. His challenge was to find ways to renew himself and persevere despite life's absurdities. It was up to him to transcend this devastating sense of meaninglessness.

People have free will and can be participants, not just observers, in their own lives.

Alexander figured out that one of life's paradoxes is that we come closer to ourselves only when we stop running away; that we must avoid "dying" while we are still living. With this insight, and after some experimentation, Alexander concluded that activities like self-development, nurturing strong friendships, engaging in community, and exploring spiritual matters were the things that made him feel truly alive.

As a first step in his journey towards change, Alexander concluded that his marriage was important to him and that time was running out to rebuild this relationship. His second major decision concerned his work. It was clear to him that it was time to leave the startup, as it no longer brought him any sense of satisfaction.

One of life's paradoxes is that we come closer to ourselves only when we stop running away; that we must avoid "dying" while we are still living.

By making these two decisions, Alexander turned the corner from despair. After descending into what he called his "lower depths," he realized that feel-ing comfortable in his own skin required meaningful relationships, a sense of community, and a pursuit of something he found truly meaningful. He dis-covered that what he truly loved—and excelled at—was uplifting others and helping people develop. Participating in such activities allowed him to create a sense of purpose and move beyond feelings of despair, as Sartre put it.

Although he knew that the difference he made might be small—perhaps even insignificant—it gave him a sense of meaning. That was his way of coping with the narcissistic injury of his own mortality and creating the illusion of being somewhat special. Making others feel special, in turn, made him feel truly alive. This led him to the decision to run a large charity for children.

Alexander was fortunate to have a good friend who supported him in his search for meaning. However, in most instances, dealing with an existential crisis requires the help of a psychotherapist or coach. This journey toward redefining life and its meaning often leads to a search for spiritual or religious answers. While a spiritual approach may not always involve traditional religious belief in God, it very often leads people in that direction.

> The therapist's challenge is to remove the psychological blockages that got their clients stuck in the first place, while helping them revive relationships or form new ones.

The usual triggers for an existential crisis include significant life events such as psychological trauma, marriage and marital issues, separations, major losses, the death of a loved one, life-threatening experiences, new relationships, substance abuse, being fired, the empty-nest syndrome, or reaching a personally significant age (leading to what is known as an anniversary reaction—a time marker reminding us of our mortality). In their work with clients, psychotherapists incorporate these factors and help individuals find their potential for growth and development. The therapist's challenge is to remove the psychological blockages that got their clients stuck in the first place, while helping them revive relationships or form new ones.

> Helping professionals assist in the search for meaning, helping clients to reclaim personal freedom and face life's vicissitudes.

Whatever helping professionals do, their work relies heavily on understanding the worldview and mental state of those they serve, including their values and belief systems. They explore current issues and concerns, placing them in a broader perspective. They help individuals see life's paradoxes and guide them toward acceptance. Most importantly, they assist in the search for meaning, helping clients to reclaim personal freedom and face life's vicissitudes.

They also support coping with any feelings of loss. As Shakespeare wisely said:

Wise men ne'er sit and wail their loss,
But cheerly seek how to redress their harms.[11]

NOTES

1 Jacobus Johannes Leeuw (1928). *The Conquest of Illusion.* New York: A. A. Knopf.

2 Jean de la Bruyère (1885/1688). Of Opinions. In *The "Characters" of Jean de la Bruyère.* Trans. Henri van Laun. London: John C. Nimmo.

3 Plato (2000/c. 399–387 BC). The apology. In *The Trial and Death of Socrates: Euthyphro, Apology, Crito, Death Scene from Phaedo.* Trans. G.M.A. Grube. Indianapolis, IN: Hackett Publishing.

4 Franklin D. Roosevelt (1933). First Inaugural Address of Franklin D. Roosevelt, Saturday March 4, 1933. https://avalon.law.yale.edu/20th_century/froos1.asp

5 Plato (1966). *Apology, Vol. 1.* Trans. by Harold North Fowler. Cambridge, MA: Harvard University Press, 29b.

6 Jean-Paul Sartre (1977/1943). *No Exit & The Flies.* Trans. Stuart Gilbert. New York: Alfred A. Knopf.

7 Alfred Lord Tennyson (1876/1850). *In Memoriam.* London: Henry S. King and Co., Section LXXIII.

8 Manfred F. R. Kets de Vries (2021). *Quo Vadis? The Existential Challenges of Leaders.* London: Palgrave Macmillan.

9 Marcus Aurelius (2006/170–180 AD). *Meditations.* Trans. with notes Martin Hammond. Harmondsworth, UK: Penguin, Book 7, meditation 46.

10 Haruki Murakami (2002/1999–2000). Landscape with flatiron. In *after the quake.* Trans. Jay Rubin. New York: Knopf.

11 William Shakespeare (c. 1591). *Henry VI, Part III*, Act V, scene 4, line 1.

14

THE DENIAL OF DEATH

Meanwhile the trees were just as green as before; the birds sang and the sun shone as clearly now as ever. The familiar surroundings had not darkened because of her grief, nor sickened because of her pain.

She might have seen that what had bowed her head so profoundly—the thought of the world's concern at her situation—was founded on an illusion. She was not an existence, an experience, a passion, a structure of sensations, to anybody but herself.

—Thomas Hardy[1]

Oh, well has it been said, that there is no grief like the grief which does not speak!

—Henry Wadsworth Longfellow[2]

In the previous chapter, I touched upon the major loss we all face: death. As discussed, some people use "manic" work activities to ward off this unpleasant thought, becoming hyperactive in their work life. Here, I continue to explore the human tendency to deny death. In this context, it is worth reflecting on a statement made by the Dalai Lama: "Analysis of death is not for the sake of becoming fearful but to appreciate this precious lifetime."[3] Indeed, awareness of death makes life all the more precious.

Awareness of death makes life all the more precious.

Reflecting on our time on Earth, a wit once summarized the seven ages of humankind as: spills, drills, thrills, bills, ills, pills, and wills. As we move beyond the mid-stage of life and are reminded of the shadow of death, the

DOI: 10.4324/9781003651260-16

endgame of ills, pills, and wills becomes more of a reality. We become more aware of our mortality, understanding that getting older is, indeed, not for the faint of heart.

What may intensify existential death anxiety is not only the fear of our own death but also that of losing loved ones. We may ask ourselves how well equipped we are to endure the loss of those close to us. Can we cope when they are no longer there? This reflection can trigger deeper self-examination, leading to existential questions like: "Why do people die?" "Why is this happening to me?" and "Life isn't fair." It may also raise broader questions such as: "Who am I?" and "Why am I here?" Finally, we might wonder: "If I am doomed to die, what's the point of living?" and "Could it be that my life has a greater purpose?"

A wit once summarized the seven ages of humankind as: spills, drills, thrills, bills, ills, pills, and wills. As we move beyond the mid-stage of life and are reminded of the shadow of death, the endgame of ills, pills, and wills becomes more of a reality.

While death may seem like a distant rumor to the young, the older we get, the more we are reminded of the inevitable march of time. We begin to realize that death is just around the corner. A stark reminder of this is seeing the people from our cohort—the generation we grew up with—pass away. Many of those we've known are dead or dying. This isn't just about people we know personally, but also those who were part of our cultural landscape.

When we hear the news that people from our cohort have died, it becomes clear that we are witnessing a never-ending vanishing act.

When we hear the news that these people have died, it becomes clear that we are witnessing a never-ending vanishing act. Consciously or unconsciously, the death of others affects us deeply. What sets humans apart from animals is our capacity to mourn people we've never met. Their death is a grim reminder of our death foretold. Depending on how important that person was in our inner life, their death can diminish our own vitality, casting a shadow over our own existence.

What sets humans apart from animals is our capacity to mourn people we've never met.

In addition to the loss of those who have passed, we are often confronted with sad news about people in a holding pattern—those for whom death seems imminent due to a terminal illness, a cruel visitor that can't be kept at bay. Hearing about those at death's door is a stark reminder of the fragility of life and that something similar could happen to us. Seeing these individuals, mere shadows of their former selves, as they battle terminal illness, can be a very sobering experience. No wonder that as we age, most people become acutely aware of the ebb and flow of time, with the dark clouds of death encroaching upon life. We begin to ask ourselves when it will be our turn in this deadly lottery. When will our number be drawn?

Despite our ability to repress unwanted thoughts, the imagery surrounding death has long shaped our associations of what we imagine the Grim Reaper might look like. Throughout human history, death imagery has been ever-present, perhaps dating back to the earliest days of *Homo sapiens*. For instance, in ancient Greek mythology, the figure of Thanatos personified death. Thanatos, under the command of Hades (the god of the dead), was responsible for carrying humans to the underworld once their time, determined by the Fates—three sisters, also called the Moirai, who personified destiny—had run out.

> Despite our ability to repress unwanted thoughts, the imagery surrounding death has long shaped our associations of what we imagine the Grim Reaper might look like.

Inspired by Greek mythology, French illustrator Gustave Doré famously portrayed Charon, the ferryman of the underworld, in one of his drawings.[4] In this depiction, Charon is seen rowing souls across the Styx to the Isle of the Dead. The image shows an old man, clad in tattered garments, with haggard cheeks and an unkempt beard, fiercely guiding his boat with a long pole. In fact, the word Charon comes from the Greek word for "fierce gaze."

In the Low Countries (the Netherlands and Belgium), death was personified as *Magere Hein* ("Meager Hein"), usually depicted as a robed skeleton wielding a scythe. This figure would cause death by coming to collect a person's soul. The word "meager" refers to its skeletal appearance, an image largely influenced by the Dance of Death (or *Danse Macabre*), a Christian motif that was widespread across Europe during the Middle Ages.[5]

> In the Middle Ages, the constant threat of a sudden and painful death seemed to have increased the religious desire for penance. At the same time, it fueled a frantic desire for amusement when it was still possible, creating the notion of a "last dance" as a form of cold comfort.

During that period, the *Visions of the Knight Tondal* was one of the most-read manuscripts.[6] The illuminations accompanying the story helped people imagine what Hell was like. This document predated the vivid and terrifying depictions of Hell found in Dante's *Divine Comedy*. The story of Tondal describes the life of a wealthy, wayward Irish knight whose soul goes on a journey through Hell and Paradise, guided by an angel. After this harrowing experience, Tondal is spiritually transformed and vows to live a more pious life. The Dutch painter Hieronymus Bosch's nightmarish portrayals of Hell appear to have been influenced by this work, offering terrifying visions of what death might entail.

In some tales about death, people attempt to avoid its arrival or fend it off. A famous example is the Buddhist parable of the mustard seed. It tells the story of a woman named Kisa Gotami, whose only child, a very young son, had died. Unwilling to accept his death, she carried his body from neighbor to neighbor, begging that someone would give her medicine to bring him back to life. One neighbor, seeing how distraught she was, suggested that she visit the Buddha, who was nearby, to ask if he could restore her son.

Carrying her son's body, Kisa found the Buddha and pleaded with him to bring her son back to life. Instead, the Buddha suggested she embark on a journey to gather mustard seeds from a household that had never been touched by death. He assured her that from those mustard seeds, he could create a medicine to restore her son. Relieved by his words, she went searching for these mustard seeds.

But wherever Kisa went, be it to hovels or palaces, the story was the same. Everyone was willing to give her some mustard seeds, but each household had been touched by death. She heard countless tales of sadness and loss. Time and again, she was reminded, "The living are few, but the dead are many."

Gradually, Kisa saw the universality of death. She came to accept that death is not the opposite of life, but an integral part of it. With this new understanding, her grief began to recede. She buried her son in the forest and returned to the Buddha. She explained that she couldn't collect the mustard seeds as instructed because she couldn't find a single household untouched by death.

Kisa soon realized that no one was better able to help these poor unfortunate people than she, having suffered misfortune herself. Armed with this insight, she became so involved in comforting others in their grief that she forgot her own quest for the magical mustard seeds. By helping others, she was able to alleviate some of her own sorrow. This story illustrates that the fear of death can be lessened by focusing on larger existential questions and accepting that death will come for us all.

> The fear of death can be lessened by focusing on larger existential questions and accepting that death will come for us all.

THE SEQUENCE OF LIFE

An essential part of human existence is the passing of generations. There is a natural sequence to life: parents should die before their children, and grandparents before the parents. Our language emphasizes this timely sequence. When parents die, their children become orphans. When a spouse dies, the surviving partner is called a widow or widower. But when a child dies, there is no specific term for the bereaved parents. Could it be that this break in the natural sequence leaves parents so overwhelmed with grief that no words exist to describe their loss?

It is always hard to imagine how we will grieve. When death visits us, what will we do? How will we cope? These questions are difficult to answer. Dealing with death has so many facets. When someone close to us dies, not only do we feel abandoned, but we also feel apprehensive as to how we will manage without them. No matter how prepared we think we are, it always comes as a shock. We can never truly prepare for such an event. After all, there is no manual for grief.

> When parents die, their children become orphans. When a spouse dies, the surviving partner is called a widow or widower. But when a child dies, there is no specific term for the bereaved parents.

Thinking about the natural sequence of life—and knowing what lies ahead—we may engage in preparatory grieving, especially for those close to us. Yet, despite our efforts to prepare for the inevitable, we have no real idea how we will grieve until the time comes. Often, when that time arrives, there is a stark difference between what we expect and what actually happens. The sudden emptiness, the realization that someone we love is gone, is hard to fathom. With death comes the painful understanding that they will be missing from our future. We grieve not only their presence but also the loss of our future together.

> We have no real idea how we will grieve until the time comes.

When this fact really sinks in, we may be overwhelmed by shock, confusion, and waves of sadness or depression. Furthermore, as sorrow rages inside us, parents might also wonder how their children will experience grief. How will they manage this sorrow?

A staged process?

Various theories attempt to describe how we react to loss and death, and how we cope with grief. Some conceptual thinkers believe that the emotions experienced by those who grieve are predictable and that grief can be monitored, almost as if ticking off a specific checklist. One such framework is the five stages of grief that were introduced by Swiss-American psychiatrist Elisabeth Kübler-Ross.[7] It's most likely that her model was influenced by the theoretical contributions of British psychoanalyst John Bowlby, who described the grieving process in terms of attachment behavior. He suggested that in the case of loss, people go through stages of protest, despair, and detachment.[8]

Kübler-Ross elaborated on this idea, proposing a five-stage model starting with denial ("This can't have happened to me."), followed by anger ("Why is this happening? Who is responsible?"), then bargaining ("Please, don't let this happen. I will do anything."), moving into depression ("I'm too upset to do anything."), and finally reaching acceptance ("I have accepted what happened.").

But grieving isn't a linear process we can map out and follow. Grieving isn't that straightforward. In grief, there is not necessarily a beginning, a middle, and an end. It is not a simple route with a destination. It is an unpredictable path with many surprises on the way. In fact, grief is much more like a roller coaster. On this journey, there will be good days and bad days. We can experience all kinds of difficult and unexpected emotions, from shock or anger to disbelief, guilt, and profound sadness. While grappling with the loss of a loved one, we might feel enveloped by a cloud of melancholia, with depression looming nearby.

> Grieving isn't a linear process we can map out and follow. It is not a simple route with a destination. It is an unpredictable path with many surprises on the way. In fact, grief is much more like a roller coaster.

What can make the grieving process so exhausting is how hard it is to control. There will be days when we feel able to cope with the loss and days when we're totally despondent. In many ways, grief is like an open sore. It doesn't simply go away, but instead changes over time. And what's more, grief will change us.

> In many ways, grief is like an open sore. It doesn't simply go away, but instead changes over time. And what's more, grief will change us.

We also need to accept that everyone grieves differently. In fact, because every relationship is unique, no two people will grieve in the same way. Each of us will have their own rhythm of suffering. Consequently, if someone's reaction to grief seems strange to us, it doesn't mean that they don't care—we just need to accept that their response is different. This applies to both the nature of the reaction and the time frame. Grief has no time limit; it has no expiration date. While the initial shock may wear off, grieving is never truly complete. Speaking from personal experience, I had engaged in preparatory grieving for my parents, particularly since they lived very long lives. Still, their death, and my very strong emotional reaction when it happened, took me by surprise.

> Grief has no time limit; it has no expiration date. While the initial shock may wear off, grieving is never truly complete.

When people die, even after the best of relationships, we often turn to memory lane. We're flooded with recollections, contributing to our feelings of sadness. We may replay fragments of our relationship with the departed over and over, reaffirming the connection we had with them. Often, we also ask ourselves what more we could have done. We may regret missed opportunities or moments where we may have been too self-centered. These recollections can fill us with sadness and unending pain.

> No two people will grieve in the same way. Each of us will have their own rhythm of suffering.

If our relationship with the deceased was difficult, this can add another dimension to our sorrow. We may suffer from a lack of closure. Whatever situation we find ourselves in, however, it will take a long time and much soul-searching before we can begin to heal from the loss.

THE LONG GOODBYE

A strong reminder of the reality of death can be the simple and everyday act of saying goodbye to those we love. It can carry a sense of foreboding, reminding us that there is going to be a final goodbye. Naturally, we try to push these thoughts away, as dwelling on them might become too stressful. If we reflected on all the last goodbyes and farewells we've experienced, we would never stop grieving. Yet, unconsciously, these goodbyes can be viewed as practice sessions for the things to come.

What really made me aware of these feelings were my visits to my mother. Sadly enough, these visits were rather infrequent, as I was living on another continent. Of course, why I lived so far away is another question. There are always rational reasons for how things turn out the way they do. Still, whatever the reasons were for the physical distance, being far from her contributed to much self-flagellation.

A strong reminder of the reality of death can be the simple and everyday act of saying goodbye to those we love. It can carry a sense of foreboding, reminding us that there is going to be a final goodbye.

When I let all these goodbyes to my mother pass through my mind, I'm still haunted by the vivid memories of her standing on the balcony of her small beachside apartment, waving at me. She looked so frail. Every time I saw her standing there, I felt immensely sad. She seemed so lonely, so abandoned. I always wondered, as I waved back, whether this would be the last time. And I always felt that I had let her down by not being more present.

In many ways, I saw those goodbyes as practice for the inevitable long goodbye. And eventually, it happened. The last goodbye became a reality. What haunts me most was that I wasn't there when she died. I arrived one day too late. I had delayed my arrival, having returned sick from an expedition in the Altai Mountains of Siberia. Sadly, I realized that there were so many more things I wished I had said, so many questions I would have liked to ask.

Realizing that both of my parents are gone still surprises me. To exist in the world while those who made me no longer do feels surreal. Their deaths taught me that coping with loss is a lifelong challenge and that I should make the most of the time I spend with those I feel close to. So much was left unsaid with my mother and father that it reminded me to tell others how much they mean to me. After all, the most painful goodbyes are the ones left unsaid.

Realizing that both of my parents are gone still surprises me. To exist in the world while those who made me no longer do feels surreal.

Waving goodbye has become an ingrained ritual for me, a way of reaffirming that death hasn't yet visited. It brings to life the French saying "*partir c'est mourir un peu*" (leaving is dying a little). It also explains why goodbyes have become so emotionally loaded—they carry a much deeper meaning. This calls to mind the English novelist George Eliot's statement that in every parting, there is an image of death.[9] Now, when I am deeply attached to someone, saying goodbye is no longer simple; it goes much deeper. Loving someone brings a sense of sadness, as we stand closest to the shadow of parting. It creates a host of associations, showing me how easily emotional bonds can be ended.

The most painful goodbyes are the ones left unsaid.

For many, reminders of the long goodbye take different forms. In my case, both homes are filled with photographs of people who were important to me. These pictures, often of family gatherings, show everyone smiling at the camera. But beneath those smiles lies a quiet sorrow, as many of those faces are no longer here. These photographs, once joyful, now reflect the tragic transience of things and the awful finality of death.

Finding closure

The American author Harriet Beecher Stowe noted, "The bitterest tears shed over graves are for words left unsaid and deeds left undone."[10] Sometimes, the hardest goodbyes are the ones never spoken—the ones that linger like a dark cloud. There's so much to say, but no one to hear it, as the one we most want to speak to is already gone. For me, I think about the many people in the generation before mine. So many unanswered questions. So many riddles. So many more things I wish I had said but never did. Now it's too late. There's no one left to answer my questions or receive my gratitude for what they did. No one left to help me navigate the unknowns. They are all gone.

The hardest goodbyes are the ones never spoken—the ones that linger like a dark cloud.

At times, the inability to do so fills me with sorrow and creates a kind of painful longing. Some of these memories turn into wounds so deep, they don't even seem to bleed. For me, this often leads to imaginary discussions with those who have passed on. Of course, I know that I can't argue with the dead. No matter what I say, they will always have the last word. Yet, while death ends a life, it doesn't end a relationship, which continues to wrestle in the mind of the survivor, seeking some final resolution or meaning that may never come. Finding closure while those we love are still alive would bring a much greater peace of mind.

> I think about the many people in the generation before mine. So
> many unanswered questions. So many riddles. So many more things
> I wish I had said but never did. Now it's too late. Some memories of
> the dead turn into wounds so deep, they don't even seem to bleed.

Recognizing the fragility of life and the power of memory, we must remind ourselves to treat others in ways that will leave no regrets. This is why the ability to forgive is so crucial. Closure is essential. It means having meaningful conversations with those close to us while there is still time. I've come to realize how important it is to make that effort. In fact, it serves both parties. Once someone is gone, it's too late for the conversations we've been putting off. Imaginary conversations with the departed may have value, but they can never fully satisfy.

> Imaginary conversations with the departed may have value, but
> they can never fully satisfy. I know that I can't argue with the
> dead. No matter what I say, they will always have the last word.

THE EXPERIENCES OF GRIEF AND MOURNING

Grief and mourning are common terms used to describe the feelings and behaviors following the loss of loved ones. While often used interchangeably, grief and mourning represent different aspects of loss. Grief refers to the internal experience—the thoughts and emotions that arise after a loss. It is numbness, sadness, anger, and regret, all intertwined. It is the deep pain within the soul, the longing to be with the person who is no longer there.

> Recognizing the fragility of life and the power of memory, we must
> remind ourselves to treat others in ways that will leave no regrets.

While grief is a personal emotional response to loss, mourning refers to the outward expressions or signs of that grief. It concerns the way we express and release our pain. Mourning is the more public process of dealing with the loss, often shaped by cultural expectations and practices. We mourn through talking about our grief, crying, writing, and using art or music to express our feelings.

With respect to mourning, societies have created many different rituals for those who have passed. But while recognizing the importance of these funeral rituals, we can also ask ourselves whether these rituals are about comforting the souls of the departed or more about consoling those left behind. Can anything really be done to help the departed? Can we truly put our dead to rest, or are these rituals primarily for our own solace?

While grief is a personal emotional response to loss, mourning refers to the outward expressions or signs of that grief.

Despite the importance of funeral rituals, in the survivors' imaginations, those who were close to us remain very much alive. Our waking moments and dreams are filled with reminders of their presence. In truth, those we love are not truly gone until we forget them. They are not dead as long as their names are still spoken.

Whatever can be said about mourning and grieving, they are always heart-breaking experiences. Accepting that someone close to us is gone is an extremely difficult task. We're left wondering how to fill the void. Grief often infiltrates our thoughts, seeping into all aspects of daily life. And just when we think we've come to terms with a loved one's departure, those devastating feelings of loss may hit us all over again. Anniversaries, holidays, and other milestones tend to reawaken memories and emotions. At any moment, memories may emerge from hidden corners of our mind, bringing back disappointments, missed opportunities, and distress. Sorrows we thought were long forgotten mix with fresh wounds.

At any moment, memories may emerge from hidden corners of our mind, bringing back disappointments, missed opportunities, and distress. Sorrows we thought were long forgotten mix with fresh wounds.

Taking myself as an example, so many years have gone by, yet there are still moments when I instinctively reach for the phone to call my mother or father. Even after all these years, their (expired) phone numbers remain in my diary, and I can't bring myself to erase them.

We will never stop grieving the people who have been important to us because we will never stop loving them. Although people die, our relationship with them does not, even as it changes over time. As painful as it is to reflect on the loss of those close to me, I realize it's part of the human condition. The Buddhist story of the mustard seed reminds us that no one escapes this sorrow. Despite my heroic attempt at preparatory grieving, the reality is that we can never be fully prepared for grief. In the end, I was given a crash course.

> We will never stop grieving the people who have been important to us because we will never stop loving them.

When death strikes, we must reassess our view of the world and our place in it. As interconnected human beings, we are not islands unto ourselves. We're connected to others by many shared experiences. In that respect, grief and memory go together. The past remains ever-present. After someone dies, memories are all we have left. It also may explain why, when our identity has been utterly wrapped up with the deceased, it becomes more difficult to deal with their loss. And if the relationship was especially intense, finding closure can feel nearly impossible.

> When our identity has been utterly wrapped up with the deceased, it becomes more difficult to deal with their loss.

Grief is what makes us human. Grief is what leads to human tragedy. Paradoxically, grief is also intertwined with love. In other words, if we can love, we are also subject to grief. In this way, grief and love are like twins, woven together from the start. But grief is a strange kind of love—it's the ultimate unrequited love. No matter how deeply we continue to love someone who has passed, they can never love us back.

Perhaps, in our strange imagination, there are no natural deaths. Deep down, every death can feel like a murder, as if life has been unfairly stolen from a loved one. Given the nature of human existence, all of us will experience and be profoundly affected by these imagined murders.

> Grief is a strange kind of love—it's the ultimate unrequited love. No matter how deeply we continue to love someone who has passed, they can never love us back.

COPING WITH GRIEF

The French philosopher Voltaire said, "Tears are the silent language of grief."[11] With this statement, he may have implied that grief cannot be ignored; it must be processed in one way or another. However, the process is challenging. It takes a lot of strength to work our way through grief and re-enter life. When we lose someone we love, we can't imagine that we will ever feel better.

In trying to rebuild our lives, we often rely on various defense mechanisms to cope with loss. From a survival standpoint, this is logical. In fact, to a degree, we all engage in self-deception. Often, we try to lock our grief away, sealing it off, but as many of us learn the hard way, suppressing grief isn't the answer. Worse still, unresolved grief can resurface unexpectedly and create complications such as depression, anxiety, and other mental health challenges. It may also contribute to substance abuse. Since grief is tied to love, the inability to grieve can also affect our capacity to love.

Grief, no matter where it comes from, can only be resolved through connection with others. We may need to rekindle old relationships or form new ones. We must heal and rebuild ourselves around the loss that we've suffered.

> Since grief is tied to love, the inability to grieve can also affect our capacity to love.

People's reactions to those who are grieving can vary widely. In some cases, others can be a source of comfort, helping to ease feelings of loss. However, people may also withdraw, seemingly afraid of being "contaminated" by grief. They may fear the intensity of the grieving person's suffering. Most likely, they may be concerned that other people's grief will stir up too many painful memories of their own.

Generally speaking, one person's grief is hard for others to grasp. Still, when faced with grieving people, we must try to honor their grief. While grieving is a lonely process, that doesn't mean others can't offer support. In fact, grief shared is often grief lessened. When we share in each other's sorrow, we may help lighten the burden. Although the grief journey is deeply personal, it is up to us to decide just how lonely it will feel. To live a life well lived, those who grieve must make an effort to become whole once more, even though they will never be quite the same again.

> Although the grief journey is deeply personal, it is up to us to decide just how lonely it will feel.

This element of personal change due to grief also raises the question of whether personal growth is possible without grief and sorrow. Could it be that there is much to learn from these painful experiences? Is the sense of loss tied to personal growth? Does suffering, in fact, fuel creativity?

As paradoxical as it may sound, there may indeed be value in suffering. Strangely, it could very well be that learning to cope with grief is part of personal growth. Despite the trauma of loss, and though we never truly outgrow it, we can still move forward and learn from it. Still, grief remains a very cruel teacher. Reflecting on my own relationship with my parents and others close to me, grieving for them has given me a deeper knowledge of who they were, how they shaped my life, and how they helped make me who I am today. But I must admit, the coping process has been incredibly challenging. In my experience, those dead who were close to me will continue to die, over and over, for the rest of my life. Their memories will always be part of me, drawing me back like a magnet. Although I may have no choice but to accept death, there is no death in remembrance. The art of living is a very delicate dance between holding on and letting go. Managing the loss of people that have been close, will always be extremely challenging.

In my experience, those dead who were close to me will continue to die, over and over, for the rest of my life. Their memories will always be part of me, drawing me back like a magnet.

NOTES

1 Thomas Hardy (1891). *Tess of the D'Urbervilles*. London: James R. Osgood, McIlvaine & Co.
2 Henry Wadsworth Longfellow (1839). A colloquy. In *Hyperion*, Book II, Chapter II. New York: Samuel Colman.
3 Bstan-'dzin-rgya-mtsho, Dalai Lama XIV (2002). *Advice on Dying and Living a Better Life*. Trans. and Ed. Jeffrey Hopkins. New York: Atria Books.
4 Dante Alighieri. *Inferno*. Plate 9.
5 Clearly, in those days, the constant threat of a sudden and painful death—most notably during the Black Death, a bubonic plague pandemic—seemed to have increased the religious desire for penance. At the same time, it fueled a frantic desire for amusement when it was still possible, creating the notion of a "last dance" as a form of cold comfort.
6 Simon Marmion (Flemish, active 1450–1489) and David Aubert (Flemish, active 1453–1479). *Les Visions du chevalier Tondal* (1475). www.getty.edu/art/collection/object/103RWK
7 Elisabeth Kübler-Ross (1969). *On Death and Dying*. New York: Macmillan.
8 John Bowlby (1969). *Attachment. Attachment and Loss: Vol. 1. Loss*. New York: Basic Books.
9 "In every parting there is an image of death." George Eliot (1864/1857). Amos Barton. In *Scenes of Clerical Life and Silas Marner*. Edinburgh and London: William Blackwood and Sons.
10 Harriet Beecher Stowe (1866). Repression. In *Little foxes: or, The Insignificant Little Habits Which Mar Domestic Happiness*. London: Bell and Daldy.
11 Voltaire (1824/1764). Tears. In *A Philosophical Dictionary from the French of M. de Voltaire*. London: J. and H. L. Hunt, Volume VI.

15

MONO NO AWARE
THE TRANSIENCE OF LIFE

Dear darling, put my hand on my heart; Oh, do you hear how noisy it is in this little room. Here is where an unpleasant carpenter dwells, He is making a coffin for me. He is hammering and knocking day and night; He keeps me from sleeping. Oh! hurry up, master carpenter, so that I can sleep.

—Heinrich Heine[1]

The boundaries which divide life from death are at best shadowy and vague. Who shall say where the one ends, and where the other begins?

—Edgar Allan Poe[a]

Everything passes away—suffering, pain, blood, hunger, pestilence. The sword will pass away too, but the stars will remain when the shadows of our presence and our deeds have vanished from the Earth. There is no man who does not know that. Why, then, will we not turn our eyes toward the stars? Why?

—Mikhail Bulgakov[3]

As discussed in the previous chapter, our denial of death underscores the impermanence of life and the inevitability of loss. Of all the losses we endure, death is the ultimate one, making us acutely aware of life's transience. The Japanese phrase *mono no aware* (pronounced moh-noh noh ah-wah-reh), which means the fleeting, tragic nature of things, captures this sense of impermanence. It serves as a reminder that from the moment we are born, we are already moving toward death. Its shadow follows us wherever we go, whatever we do.

DOI: 10.4324/9781003651260-17

But death remains an unwanted visitor. When it arrives, will we be prepared? Will the thought of our impending death paralyze us? As I've also suggested, the reality of death as our final destination should never be an excuse to stop living. In fact, without death, life would have no boundaries. It is the finite nature of our days that makes them so much more precious.

The reality of death as our final destination
should never be an excuse to stop living.

The awareness of our own mortality stems from the development of our frontal lobes—the last part of the human brain to mature fully. Unlike other species in the animal kingdom, *Homo sapiens* is "blessed" with higher mental faculties, allowing us not only to live in the present but also to ponder the future. While having a well-developed brain can be a blessing, it can also be a curse. Our ability to look ahead and remember the tragic finiteness of life can create a dark cloud always hovering above us—the heavy price our species pays for its evolutionary success.

Carrying the burden of knowing that we are mortal can make us fearful of what lies beyond. For many, death is like a black hole, the end of all experience. It evokes a sense of nothingness, a fear of the dark abyss, and the permanent extinction of being. Lurking beneath our consciousness, this uncertainty is inherently difficult to manage.

Unlike other species in the animal kingdom, *Homo sapiens* is
"blessed" with higher mental faculties, allowing us not only to
live in the present but also to ponder the future.

This difficulty reminds me of the ancient Babylonian tale "Appointment in Samarra." It tells of a merchant in Baghdad who sent his servant to the market to buy provisions. Soon after, the servant returned, pale and trembling. He said, "Master, when I was in the marketplace, I was pushed by a woman in the crowd. When I turned, I realized that it was Death who had accosted me. She looked at me and made a threatening gesture. I am so scared. Please lend me one of your horses so I can ride far away from this city and escape my fate. I will go to Samarra. Death will not find me there."

The merchant lent his servant a horse, and the servant rode as fast as he could towards Samarra. After he had gone, the merchant went to the marketplace and saw Death standing in the crowd. He approached and asked, "Why did you make such a threatening gesture to my servant when you saw him this morning?"

Death responded, "It was not a threatening gesture at all. It was a gesture of surprise. I was amazed to see him in Baghdad, for I have an appointment with him tonight in Samarra."

Clearly, some of us will face our appointment with death sooner than others. But what we all have in common is that this appointment is inevitable. Given the uncertainty of what lies beyond, it's no wonder we go to great lengths to distract ourselves from this unpleasant reality. But is that the way to move forward? Is that how we should view life? Not at all. Despite our efforts to push thoughts of death out of consciousness, we better learn to accept that there's no living without dying. As I've mentioned before, it is death that gives life its true meaning.

Clearly, some of us will face their appointment with death sooner than others. But what we all have in common is that this appointment is inevitable.

Symbolically, for many people, death can be seen as the ultimate narcissistic injury. While we may rationally understand that death is part of the cycle of life, our irrational selves tend to view it very differently. For many people, the idea of disappearing into a void—the disintegration and decay of our body—is hard to accept. None of us wants to believe in our own personal demise. The prospect of nothingness, where the self ceases to exist, is, given our psychological makeup, almost incomprehensible. It's no surprise that death anxiety causes much (conscious and unconscious) discomfort that manifests through an array of affective, cognitive, developmental, and socio-cultural reactions.

DEALING WITH DEATH ANXIETY

As the saying goes, human beings fall from womb to tomb. Or, in the words of American psychologist William James, death is "the worm at the core" of our existence.[4] From our first breath, we are set on the path to death. Our ability to anticipate ensures that thoughts of death always linger. The challenge of the human condition lies in how we confront the terror of death, which, with all its mystery, often leaves us questioning the purpose of life.

From our first breath, we are set on the path to death.

Given my advanced age, I've become very aware of life's endpoint. As the Bible states, our allotted life span is "threescore years and ten." Clearly,

I have passed that mark. Now, each birthday becomes a disturbing reminder of milestones past. Obituaries play a similar role. These days, when I read them, I always notice the age of the deceased, and I instinctively compare it with my own. What's particularly disquieting is that many are younger than me. It makes me wonder how much time I have left and how prepared I am for the endpoint.

For young people, death is a distant rumor. But for people my age, that's no longer the case. As the ranks of my age group thin out, it's become increasingly difficult for me to hold on to the fantasy that I have much time left. The death announcements—very rare in my younger days—have turned into an avalanche. They constantly remind me to make the most of the time I have left. And even though I understand death is inevitable, I also know that when it comes, it may still catch me by surprise.

> Even though I understand death is inevitable, I also know that when it comes, it may still catch me by surprise.

Death acceptance

Many people behave as if death is something that happens to others, clinging to the fantasy that an exception will be made for them. Their fear of the unknown turns them into experts in defensive maneuvers to keep the thought at bay. Yet, if they accepted death, they would be more prepared to live fully. Part of the challenge lies in the fear of a violent or painful death, which is why, unsurprisingly, many hope to die peacefully in their sleep.

Most people don't realize that they've already had plenty of practice dealing with death. Each night when we fall asleep, we are, in a sense, practicing for death. Before we close our eyes, there's always the question of whether we will wake up again. Could it be that time and death sleep side by side? If we felt the same about sleeping as we do about dying, the idea of death would be much less of an issue. Consequently, sleep can be seen as the twin of death.

> Each night, when we fall asleep, we are, in a sense, practicing for death.

Still, no matter how we look at it, dying well begins with accepting that death is a natural part of life. We cannot choose *not* to die. However, this doesn't mean life should be miserable or that there is no hope. In the time we are given, much can be achieved. There are positive choices we can make. We can decide where to focus our time and attention. We can choose to reach out—to connect with others or dedicate ourselves to meaningful causes. At the same time, we can look inward and come to terms with who we are and who we've been. As I have mentioned over and over again, these internal journeys can be as beneficial as external ones, bringing a deep sense of peace. After all, if there's no peace in life, there will be no peace in death. Dying well implies hard work, because dying is more than a physical process. It encompasses our whole being—physical, psychological, and spiritual.

Dying well implies hard work, because dying is more than a physical process. It encompasses our whole being—physical, psychological, and spiritual.

Since death is viewed as the ultimate loss—the loss of everything we've ever possessed—the saying about not wanting to be the richest person in the graveyard is quite apt. It reaffirms once more that death strips away all that we once valued. With death, we need to let go of all our attachments. With death, we won't be able to control our affairs. We will lose the ability to care for those who depend on us.

Of course, alongside the fear of death, there are also concerns about pain and loneliness in dying. We've all witnessed examples of this. Everyone hopes for a painless death, but too often we see the opposite. No wonder that death anxiety lies at the heart of many neurotic conflicts. Managing this fear has been a challenge as old as *Homo sapiens* itself. Many live in denial of death's patient courtship until, someday, they find it sitting at their bedside.

Historically, one popular way of pursuing immortality has been the search for the elixir of eternal youth—a potion that would make the person who drinks it immortal. This idea has been omnipresent throughout human history. Many snake oil salesmen have preyed on people's naivety in their quest for immortality. Although this pursuit is nonsensical, the longing for its equivalent persists. Today's snake oil salesmen have morphed into advocates of the life extension industry, promising similar magical cures. This industry often promotes pseudo-science, mixing grains of truth with bad science. These so-called immortality prophets suggest that, with scientific innovations, people can delay or slow the dying process through medical science, complex diets, and exercise regimens. Many also believe they can maintain the illusion of youth through plastic surgery. In reality, these life extension advocates leave a trail of false hopes, broken promises, and unfulfilled dreams.

Many live in denial of death's patient courtship until, someday, they find it sitting at their bedside.

As the famous Swiss psychoanalyst Carl Jung said, "Shrinking away from death is something unhealthy and abnormal which robs the second half of life of its purpose. Do not fear death so much but rather the inadequate life."[5] Similarly, the Roman Emperor Marcus Aurelius remarked, "It is not death that a man should fear, but he should fear never beginning to live."[6] As mentioned earlier, death is not the opposite of life but a part of it. The worst thing would be to lose our reason for living.

Death is not the opposite of life but a part of it. The worst thing would be to lose our reason for living.

Onwards with our defenses

When it comes to death, our defenses often work overtime. We prefer to flee from death's looming presence, doing everything in our power to push thoughts of it away. From a psychological perspective, however, this is exhausting work. Defenses such as repression, denial, displacement, or believing in our personal invincibility are far from seamless. Death anxiety has a way of creeping up, disguised in many forms, revealing the limits of these defensive strategies. Still, every human society has tried to create structures, symbols, narratives, and rituals to deal with it.

Beyond these defensive structures, what truly matters is whether our time on Earth has had meaning. Have we made a difference, however small, in the lives of others? On our deathbed, how we view our life will depend not only on what happened to us but also on how we responded. The peace we feel about our actions will be influenced by how we've relied on so-called "immortality systems." In a sense, these systems—ways of leaving a lasting impact—are our attempts to defy and deny death. They reflect humanity's desire to retain hope, despite the tragedy of the human condition.

IMMORTALITY SYSTEMS

Awareness of our mortality has a unique power to focus the mind and heart on what's essential. Given how difficult it is to accept the notion of death, we often fabricate the illusion of immortality. We strive to leave some kind of mark. We want to believe that something will transcend us. Our narcissistic disposition—our need to feel important in the grand scheme of things—explains why we hold on to these illusions. We do all this to ensure that our time on Earth has had meaning.

Given how difficult it is to accept the notion of death, we often fabricate the illusion of immortality. We strive to leave some kind of mark. We want to believe that something will transcend us.

From an evolutionary point of view, *Homo sapiens* realized that an obsession with mortality would be ineffective as a survival strategy. It would only hinder our evolutionary progress. As a result, the perception of symbolic immortality becomes essential to our mental health. It helps us maintain a vital and enduring sense of self. Hence, humans have been driven to find ways to process these morbid thoughts, with some strategies proving more effective than others. Without this ability, we risk falling into a depressive state, becoming dysfunctional, or—most troublingly—viewing suicide as the existential resolution.

Homo sapiens has always wishfully believed in the possibility of another life, a second act. This is what drives the widespread belief in an afterlife—whether through literal means, such as reincarnation or eternal life in heaven, or through the idea that some aspects of us will persist over time, whether through nature, children, memorable organizations, political impact, or great works of art or science. If we can put these ideas at the center of our lives, living becomes more bearable. Through meaning, we may affirm our existence. These efforts to cope with thoughts of death take many different forms.

Through meaning, we may affirm our existence.

Nature and immortality

A 4,853-year-old Great Basin bristlecone pine, known as Methuselah, stands in a secret location within the Inyo National Forest's White Mountains in California. This tree is as close to immortality as most of us will ever come. In this sense, nature itself creates hope in immortality. While each of us will be subjected to decay, the sum total of humankind—nature—can be seen as immortal. We can tell ourselves that we will never truly die because we are one with nature. We are conceived and born, then we live and die, and, after death, we decay. That's the flow of life. The Earth is the prime example of birth, growth, and renewal. It is also where we lay our dead. As our bodies decay, they nourish the earth, supporting new life in the form of insects and plants. Thus, from an ecological perspective, all of us are part of a natural immortality system.

> While each of us will be subjected to decay, the sum total of
> humankind—nature—can be seen as immortal. From an ecological
> perspective, all of us are part of a natural immortality system.

The fact that nothing dies in nature has been echoed in various religions since our Paleolithic ancestors. For example, the Hindu scriptures teach that we were formed from dust and ash. The Old Testament of the Bible reminds us, "Dust thou art, and to dust thou shalt return."[7] The Quran similarly tells us that humankind was created from dust and water. The earth may be where we lay our dead, but it is also a place of resurrection.

It's not surprising that many people feel a deep connection with nature, viewing death as a transition rather than an end. Some even experience *unio mystica*, an "oceanic feeling" of boundlessness, where they seem to merge with the universe. Symbolically, our perceptions of nature and immortality are intimately connected. Venturing into mountains, valleys, forests, rivers, and oceans is a fundamental human urge and a form of communion with life and death for many. Nature can also have a therapeutic effect, harnessed by practices like ecotherapy, which uses guided nature-based activities for healing.[8]

> Venturing into mountains, valleys, forests, rivers,
> and oceans is a fundamental human urge and a
> form of communion with life and death for many.

Returning to nature in death symbolizes how we participate in the eternal cycle of life. No wonder that many early cultures honored Gaia, the goddess of the Earth. They would find comfort and security in the daily cycle of night and day, the changing seasons, and the growth of living things. Every night that would enfold them in darkness would represent death, but with the first light of dawn, life would be renewed. Nothing in nature, not even the tiniest particle, disappears without a trace. Nature knows only transformation. In this sense, we can speak of immortality. However, due to humanity's treatment of the planet, growing concerns about its viability now cast doubt on this immortality system.

> Nothing in nature, not even the tiniest particle, disappears
> without a trace. Nature knows only transformation.

Religious systems

People seem to become more interested in places of worship as they get older. Symbolically, they may be preparing for their "final exam." It's a truism to say that the primary purpose of all religions is to address our concerns about death. Belief systems have long been humanity's most ingenious solutions for coping with mortality. To deal with death and the "whys" of existence, we construct religious meaning systems. In an exercise of wishful thinking, believers perform rituals, follow rules, and expect to be supernaturally rewarded with long life, honor, wisdom, children, health, wealth, victory, and immortality after death. No wonder that religion has always been the most common way to assure us of continuity. As American psychiatrist Irvin Yalom noted, "Death anxiety is the mother of all religions, which, in one way or another, attempt to temper the anguish of our finitude."[9] These belief systems help soothe the existential anxiety that comes with the human condition.

> It's a truism to say that the primary purpose of all religions is to address our concerns about death.

Throughout history, religion has been *Homo sapiens'* most resourceful ally in alleviating the fear of death and the annihilation of the self. The reality of human helplessness has always been difficult to bear, and in this respect, religion provides a soothing balm. It helps humanity reconcile itself to fate through the comfort of eternal life. To address prevailing anxieties, all the major world religions offer the promise of an afterlife. They also serve a consoling function and play an integrative role in society. Religious and spiritual conceptions of immortality range from the Judeo-Christian and Islamic beliefs in an afterlife and resurrection to the cycles of rebirth in Buddhism and Hinduism. Furthermore, by offering heaven as the ultimate destination, religions incentivize people to live virtuously despite life's constraints, contributing to social harmony. In this way, religions have a wish-fulfillment quality. They satisfy the universal desire for a just world—where good behavior is rewarded, and bad behavior punished—and for a realm beyond suffering.

Unfortunately, throughout human history, religious conviction has too often led to violence against those with different beliefs. Perhaps the passionate defense of one belief system over another is driven by lingering doubts—an underlying fear among believers that they may have made the wrong choice. This concern can fuel anxiety over what happens if the promised heaven or afterlife doesn't exist.

> People come and go, but by identifying with those before us and those who will come after, we seem to transcend ourselves through our ancestors and descendants.

Consequently, religious belief systems can provoke very destructive reactions. Adherents of one belief system may feel compelled to attack, degrade, or even kill those of different faiths. All too often, religious leaders incite aggression, fanaticism, hatred, and xenophobia, driven by the notion that only true believers will attain immortality. As the French mathematician-philosopher Blaise Pascal noted, "Men never do evil so completely and cheerfully as when they do it from religious conviction."[10] All the major religions are guilty of atrocities committed against one another, while various sects within these religions fight among themselves. Despite the discord, religious belief systems play a major role in addressing the fear of non-existence.

However, the question remains: Can religions deliver on their promises? Can they present evidence that the soul is immortal? If not, what do they offer in return? From a scientific perspective, if there is no hard evidence, are there still reasons to believe? Scientifically speaking, concepts like the immortality of the soul, Hell, and Paradise don't hold much weight. This suggests—again from a scientific rather than mystical viewpoint—that religions, given the evidence available, rest on a shaky foundation. If they can prove the existence of immortality or resurrection beyond death, belief would naturally follow. Without such proof, doubt will always persist.

> If religions can prove the existence of immortality
> or resurrection beyond death, belief would naturally
> follow. Without such proof, doubt will always persist.

Procreation

As mentioned before, death is an incurable disease we contract the moment we are conceived. This raises the question of whether, from a purely rational perspective, it makes sense to bring children into the world, given their inevitable fate. Yet, beyond rationality, children often become our primary immortality project. We pass on our aspirations and values to them, hoping they will carry forward our beliefs. Children help us see death as a transition, allowing us to "survive" in the memories of others. After all, the dead are never truly gone until they are forgotten. Thus, procreation becomes another natural immortality system. We hope that the passing of memories from generation to generation will create continuity, ensuring our symbolic immortality as our spirit and philosophy of life live on through our children.

> Death is an incurable disease we
> contract the moment we are conceived.

The role of creativity

When we engage in creative acts—whether through art, literature, scientific discovery, or simple acts of kindness—we also strive to create a form of symbolic immortality. In this way, we not only confront our death anxiety but also "escape" death by living on through our actions and accomplishments, which may be remembered for generations, or even centuries.

> Children help us see death as a transition, allowing
> us to "survive" in the memories of others.

Legacy creation is a major way of achieving a form of immortality. Artists hope their works will live on after them, allowing them to transcend death. Creation gives their lives meaning, as their work may benefit future generations. Similarly, scientists build cumulative knowledge and hope that others will carry their research forward—another expression of creative immortality. Entrepreneurs, too, aim for their companies to outlast them.

> When we engage in creative acts—whether through art,
> literature, scientific discovery, or simple acts of kindness—
> we also strive to create a form of symbolic immortality.

Creativity as a remedy for death anxiety can become an integral part of the search for meaning. In a similar way, actors and athletes can make history through extraordinary performances or by breaking longstanding records. All these activities symbolizing immortality are means to transcend death and live on in the memories of others.

> Creativity as a remedy for death anxiety can
> become an integral part of the search for meaning.

THE PURSUIT OF ILLUSIONS

Mortality is a universal human obsession. However, it may be that our desire for immortality doesn't stem from the fear of death, but rather that our fear of death arises from our desire for immortality. Perhaps we would truly feel immortal if we stopped worrying about death. In that sense, could it be that young people, who rarely think about death, are the ones who feel truly immortal? Of course, it could be argued that this preoccupation with immortality is merely a narcissistic pursuit; that we should know better than to pursue this avenue. As a wit once said, millions long for immortality while they don't know what to do with themselves on a rainy Sunday afternoon. Why do so many people yearn for immortality when they struggle to make the most of the brief life they already have?

> Mortality is a universal human obsession. However, it may be that our desire for immortality doesn't stem from the fear of death, but rather that our fear of death arises from our desire for immortality.

In the context of immortality, what makes sense is the fact that each of our lives is interwoven with those of others—not only in the present, but throughout time. People come and go, but by identifying with those before us and those who will come after, we seem to transcend ourselves through our ancestors and descendants. After our death, the stories people will tell about us are what will carry on. Perhaps not forever, but for some time. Through these life-defining stories, we can imagine attaining some form of immortality. If something in others comes to life because of us, we've left a trace of immortality. Yet, as we hold on to this idea, we must keep in mind that all attempts at immortality—whether through leadership, conquest, science, or the arts—are ultimately fleeting, because the "long run" is far longer than any of us can imagine.

> Why do so many people yearn for immortality when they struggle to make the most of the brief life they already have?

The Scottish novelist Robert Louis Stevenson noted, "To believe in immortality is one thing, but it is first needful to believe in life."[11] Frankly, from a realistic point of view, life is not about striving for immortality, but about accepting our mortality. Immortality, it seems, is nothing more than a strange illusion. While we may wish for more time, the key is to increase the quality of the time we do have.

> Frankly, from a realistic point of view, life is not about striving for immortality, but about accepting our mortality. While we may wish for more time, the key is to increase the quality of the time we do have.

NOTES

1 Author's translation of the original: *Lieb Liebchen, leg's Händchen aufs Herze mein; Ach, hörst du, wie's pochet im Kämmerlein? Da hauset ein Zimmermann schlimm und arg, Der zimmert mir einen Todtensarg. Es hämmert und klopfet bei Tag und bei Nacht; Es hat mich schon längst um den Schlaf gebracht. Ach! sputet Euch, Meister Zimmermann, Damit ich balde schlafen kann!* Heinrich Heine (1920/1817–1821). Junge Leiden: Leider IV. In *Buch der Leider von H. Heine.* Ed. John Lees. London: Longmans, Green & Co.

2 Edgar Allen Poe (1852/1844). The premature burial. In *Tales of Mystery, Imagination, & Humour; and Poems*. London: Henry Vizetelly.
3 Author's translation of the original: *Vse proydet. Stradaniya, muki, krov', golod i mor. Mech ischeznet, a vot zvezdy ostanutsya, kogda i teni nashikh tel i del ne ostanetsya na zemle. Net ni odnogo cheloveka, kotoryy by etogo ne znal. Tak pochemu zhe my ne khotim obratit' svoy vzglyad na nikh? Pochemu?* Mikhail Bulgakov (1929). *The White Guard [Belaia gvardiia]*. Paris: Concorde, Volume II.
4 William James (1902). *The Varieties of Religious Experience*. New York: Longmans, Green, and Co.
5 Carl Jung (1968). *Structure and Dynamics of the Psyche*. Princeton, NJ: Princeton University Press.
6 Marcus Aurelius (2007). *Meditations*. New York: Penguin.
7 Genesis 3:19.
8 Manfred F. R. Kets de Vries (2016). Eco-therapy: The Walking and Talking Cure. INSEAD Knowledge. https://knowledge.insead.edu/leadership-organisations/eco-therapy-walking-and-talking-cure
9 Irving Yalom (1980). *Existential Psychotherapy*. New York: Basic Books.
10 Blaise Pascal (2000/1670). *Pensées*. Paris: Livre de poche, no. 894.
11 Robert Louis Stevenson (2001). *The Complete Personal Essays of Robert Louis Stevenson*. London: Routledge.

16

HOW TO FACE OUR
EXISTENTIAL DILEMMAS

All life is an experiment. The more experiments you make the better.

—Ralph Waldo Emerson[1]

There are moments when one has to choose between living one's own life, fully, entirely, completely—or dragging out some false, shallow, degrading existence that the world in its hypocrisy demands.

—Oscar Wilde[2]

In dealing with existential crises pertaining to loss—especially death, the ultimate loss—it's helpful to draw on both psychology and philosophy. In fact, philosophers have often paved the way for psychologists in exploring humanity's most salient issues. Thinkers like Søren Kierkegaard, Friedrich Nietzsche, Karl Jaspers, Edmund Husserl, Martin Heidegger, Maurice Merleau-Ponty, Arthur Schopenhauer, and Jean-Paul Sartre frequently grappled with themes of emotional and mental distress.[3] In their philosophical contemplations they examined various kinds of losses associated with the human condition. They deeply considered how questions of "being" affect mental states and behavior, thereby shaping the way we live our daily lives within the framework of these existential questions.

Many psychologists, influenced by these philosophers, shared a similar outlook. They blended the big questions of philosophy within the mandate of psychology. I am referring to the contributions of thinkers such as Ludwig Binswanger, Viktor Frankl, Rollo May, R. D. Laing, and Irvin Yalom.[4] They drew heavily on philosophical ruminations as they sought to understand

DOI: 10.4324/9781003651260-18

better their clients' predicaments, paradoxes, and conflicts. These existentially oriented psychologists considerably focused on their clients' subjective experience—their sense of being (or *Dasein*, the German word for "being there"). They explored the paradox of living: existing in relation to others while ultimately being alone, combined with the realization that all existence ends in death.

> Existentially oriented psychologists explored the paradox of living:
> existing in relation to others while ultimately being alone, combined
> with the realization that all existence ends in death.

As a helping professional, much of my psychotherapeutic and coaching work revolves around these existential dilemmas—the inevitable losses we all face. In my practice, I pay much attention to the here-and-now (especially within the transferential context, where clients' reactions within therapy are based on previous relationships). Naturally, with my psychoanalytic training, I also take past life experiences into consideration. In addition, in this therapeutic exchange, I focus not only on the question of "being" but also on "becoming." The challenge for helping professionals is to encourage their clients to take ownership of their concerns and to help them navigate the feelings of loss that are part and parcel of the human condition. My role as an executive coach, psychoanalyst, or psychotherapist is to help my clients face ultimate concerns such as death, freedom, isolation, and meaninglessness.⁵

In my work with clients, I must always be wary of making normative judgments. To be effective in helping them, I adopt a non-judgmental, non-directive—yet not directionless—attitude. As we explore their feelings of loss, I encourage my clients to find out what truly matters to them and to find their own perspective and position in the world, within the parameters and limits of human existence.

> As we explore their feelings of loss, I encourage my clients to find
> out what truly matters to them and to find their own perspective
> and position in the world, within the parameters and limits
> of human existence.

Paradoxically, I also point out that life's supposed absence of meaning creates a deep need for meaning. After all, the alternative would be a descent into an existential abyss. Therefore, to address this void, I often integrate philosophical insights into my psychotherapeutic and coaching practice, helping clients explore what matters to them, often in the face of a seemingly indifferent or absurd world. Throughout this process, my goal is to foster their personal growth and resilience.

Life's supposed absence of meaning creates a deep need for meaning.

Unsurprisingly, raising awareness of mortality has always been central to my dialogue with clients. In this context, I point out that confronting, rather than denying, the inevitability of death can help them lead a more authentic and meaningful life. In addition, I reflect on the question of freedom and responsibility. I make it clear to my clients that while they are free to make choices, they must also bear the consequences of those choices. This can lead to existential anxiety, as the weight of responsibility can be daunting. However, I help my clients realize that their current state is something they've chosen, and that they can choose better, more meaningful ways of addressing their existential concerns. Furthermore, I discuss the tension between isolation and connection. As noted in Chapters 8 and 9, although humans are fundamentally alone in their experiences, they also deeply long for connection. Human beings are not islands unto themselves, but this duality between individuality and the desire for community often creates inner conflict.

Human beings are not islands unto themselves, but this duality between individuality and the desire for community often creates inner conflict.

The physical world brings both pain and pleasure, and the social world can lead to both heartbreak and loneliness, as well as love and affection. Dealing with loss is an integral part of the human condition. By helping people face these issues, I strive to create a therapeutic atmosphere that fosters self-exploration and self-discovery. In that respect, I urge my clients to confront their inner demons without resorting to primitive defenses such as splitting, projection, or denial. In addition, I may challenge them to think through the consequences of their choices (both past and future), recognize and accept their limitations as well as their possibilities, fulfill their potential, and truly own their lives. Through this existential work, I assist clients in discovering their purpose, finding motivation, and uncovering what truly matters to them.

> The physical world brings both pain and pleasure, and the
> social world can lead to both heartbreak and loneliness,
> as well as love and affection.

AUTHENTICITY AND SINCERITY

Even with guidance, facing life head-on is never easy. Coping with existential anxiety will always be a difficult task. Shakespeare, in *Macbeth*, poignantly captures this struggle:

> Life's but a walking shadow, a poor player
> That struts and frets his hour upon the stage
> And then is heard no more. It is a tale
> Told by an idiot, full of sound and fury,
> Signifying nothing.[6]

Shakespeare is right. And as the various essays in this book have made clear, we must accept that life inevitably involves a multitude of losses. These losses come in many forms, shaped by both internal and external dynamics. It is this awareness of the inevitability of loss that lends a tragic quality to human existence. Such knowledge drives us to seek community and meaning. This is why living a full life is so crucial. The real tragedy of life is not death itself, but the realization, when the time comes, that we've never truly lived but rather squandered our precious time.

> The awareness of the inevitability of loss lends a tragic
> quality to human existence.

Thus, in facing loss, we would do well to live an authentic life. In the art of living, authenticity is a recurring theme. It reflects a harmony between our inner and outer worlds—a convergence that's not a given, but a matter of choice. In contrast, when we live an inauthentic life, we often trade our individuality and responsibility for the security of blending in and not rocking the boat. This can result in a rather robotic life—one devoid of passion and meaning.

> The real tragedy of life is not death itself, but the realization,
> when the time comes, that we've never truly lived but rather
> squandered our precious time.

If we choose authenticity, we open ourselves to life's possibilities. We can live in a way that's more consistent with our true nature and core values, despite the risks, setbacks, and suffering this may entail. We recognize life's paradoxes, predicaments, and problems, yet remain true to ourselves. This means expressing our genuine thoughts, feelings, and beliefs, even when they contradict societal expectations or norms. Living authentically also brings clarity to our decision-making. However, it requires accepting that suffering is part of the human condition.

Closely related to the question of authenticity—being true to oneself—is the concept of living with sincerity. Sincerity refers to the absence of hypocrisy, meaning that we communicate and act in accordance with the entirety of our feelings, beliefs, thoughts, and desires in an honest and genuine way. Like authenticity, sincerity means expressing our thoughts and feelings in a truthful manner; speaking or acting in ways that reflect our true beliefs, feelings, or intentions.

> If we choose authenticity, we open ourselves to life's possibilities. We can live in a way that's more consistent with our true nature and core values, despite the risks, setbacks, and suffering this may entail.

True versus false self

When we are authentic and sincere, we stay true to our own personality, spirit, and character, no matter the external circumstances. We don't behave deceptively or give a false appearance of honesty. Instead, we present our true self, rooted in our authentic, genuine core identity. This leads to a sense of inner harmony, self-awareness, and self-acceptance. When our innate preferences, values, beliefs, and desires align, we experience fulfillment, purpose, and a deep sense of well-being. We feel truly alive. However, cultivating and expressing our true self often requires a journey of self-exploration and introspection.

> When we are authentic and sincere, we stay true to our own personality, spirit, and character, no matter the external circumstances.

In contrast, the false self is a defensive façade behind which we feel empty. It involves adopting a persona or identity that deviates from our genuine nature but conforms to societal expectations. It is often a way to gain approval or protect ourselves from perceived threats. From a developmental perspective, the false self can develop as a coping mechanism in response to trauma, societal pressures, or a need for acceptance. It represents behavior that is learned and controlled, rather than spontaneous and genuine. It manifests as behavior, attitudes, and expressed beliefs that don't align with our authentic self. Predictably, this disconnect leads to feelings of emptiness, inner conflict, and a sense of loss. Over time, relying heavily on the false self can result in alienation.

Cultivating and expressing our true self often requires a journey of self-exploration and introspection.

To be true to ourselves, we must stop pretending and deeply commit to transparency, honesty, and genuineness. It means being in tune with our values and passions, navigating life with purpose, and making thoughtful decisions. Living this way demands courage, patience, and perseverance. But while this may be challenging, it ultimately leads to deeper connections and a more satisfying, happier life—one where we are better equipped to deal with the inevitability of loss.

The false self is a defensive façade behind which we feel empty.

The French-American diarist Anaïs Nin once said, "Life is a process of becoming, a combination of states we have to go through. Where people fail is that they wish to elect a state and remain in it. This is a kind of death."[7] Clearly, the challenge before us is to navigate the tragic transience of life with passion, facing head-on the losses that come with it. Hence, when the coming of the night arrives, we can aim for a graceful exit. A truly graceful exit means looking back on something enduring—something to which we have contributed that is larger than ourselves. Transcending one's personal self is the most creative way to cope with the inevitable losses that life brings. Through self-exploration, while safeguarding authenticity and sincerity, we can live more fully and consciously, aligned with our true selves.

To be true to ourselves, we must stop pretending and deeply commit to transparency, honesty, and genuineness. Transcending one's personal self is the most creative way to cope with the inevitable losses that life brings.

Coming full circle

As I shared in the preface, the impulse to write about the many shades of loss began with the death of my close friend, Sudhir. His passing opened a quiet door within me—one that led to many memories of other losses, both sharp and subtle.

> The challenge before us is to navigate the tragic transience of life with passion, facing head-on the losses that come with it.

All of us cross thresholds in life where innocence yields to understanding—often at a cost. A child discovers the world is not always just; a society awakens to the hidden price of its progress. These moments shape us, yet they carry a sorrow for what cannot be reclaimed. We grieve about what we experience as loss. Here, growth and grief can be close companions.

Time, too, moves without pause or permission. With it go the dreams left untouched, the words left unsaid, the hands we failed to hold long enough. Time is a currency we spend without knowing the balance, and never with the option of refund.

> Time moves without pause or permission. With it go the dreams left untouched, the words left unsaid, the hands we failed to hold long enough. Time is a currency we spend without knowing the balance, and never with the option of refund.

Then there is the ache of separation—of loved ones lost, of identities dissolved, of chances missed, of communities torn at the seams. Even in this hyperconnected world, many of us drift in deeper loneliness. Connection, after all, is more than communication; it is belonging.

> Even in this hyperconnected world, many of us drift in deeper loneliness.

And meaning itself is not immune to erosion. In a world constantly shifting, once-stable beliefs—religions, ideologies, shared myths—may fall away. When they do, we are left to chart our own course through the silence, fashioning purpose in a cosmos that offers no easy truths.

Perhaps the deepest loss is the recognition that we are not really in control of our life. Illness, accident, the sudden twist of fate—these remind us of life's fragile architecture. And yet, it is in this vulnerability that we often find our common ground. Maybe even the root of compassion.

Grief is the thread running through it all. It doesn't end—it simply becomes something we live alongside. Like all human beings, I am learning how to live with it, day by day. And in that spirit, I turn to the words of the American author Helen Keller, who knew much of loss and love: "What we have once enjoyed we can never lose. . . . All that we love deeply becomes a part of us."[8]

NOTES

1 Ralph Waldo Emerson (1911/1842). *The Journals of Ralph Waldo Emerson. Vol. VI: 1841–1844*. Ed. Edward Waldo Emerson and Waldo Emerson Forbes. Boston, MA and New York: Houghton Mifflin Company, entry 11 November 1842.

2 Oscar Wilde (1893). *Lady Windermere's Fan*. New York and London: Samuel French.

3 Martin Heidegger (1962/1927). *Being and Time*. Trans. J. Macquarrie and E. S. Robinson. London: Harper & Row; Edmund Husserl (1977/1925). *Phenomenological Psychology*. Trans. J. Scanlon. The Hague: Nijhoff; Karl Jaspers (1964). *The Nature of Psychotherapy*. Chicago, IL: University of Chicago Press; Søren Kierkegaard (1980/1844). *The Concept of Anxiety*. Trans. R. Thomte. Princeton, NJ: Princeton University Press; Søren Kierkegaard (1941/1855). *The Sickness Unto Death*. Trans. W. Lowrie. Princeton, NJ: Princeton University Press; Maurice Merleau-Ponty (1964). *Sense and Non-Sense*. Trans. H. Dreyfus and P. Dreyfus. Evanston, IL: Northwestern University Press; Friedrich Nietzsche (1986/1878). *Human, All Too Human*. Trans. R. J. Hollingdale. Cambridge: Cambridge University Press; Friedrich Nietzsche (1933/1883). *Thus Spoke Zarathustra*. Trans. A. Tille. New York: Dutton; Jean Paul Sartre (1943). *No Exit*. Trans. S. Gilbert. New York: Knopf; Arthur Schopenhauer (2000/1818). *The World as Will and Representation, Volume I*. Trans. E. F. J. Payne. New York: Dover Publications.

4 Ludwig Binswanger (1963). *Being-in-the-World*. Trans. J. Needleman. New York: Basic Books; Victor Frankl (1967). *Psychotherapy and Existentialism*. Harmondsworth, UK: Penguin; Rollo May (1969). *Existential Psychology*. New York: Random House; Ronald Laing (1960). *The Divided Self*. London: Tavistock Publications; Irwin Yalom (1989). *Love's Executioner and Other Tales of Psychotherapy*. London: Bloomsbury Publications.

5 Irvin Yalom (1980). *Existential Psychotherapy*. New York: Basic Books.

6 William Shakespeare (c.1606). *Macbeth*, Act 5, Scene 5, lines 17–28.

7 Evelyn J. Hinz (1971). *The Mirror and the Garden: Realism and Reality in the Writings of Anaïs Nin*. New York: Harcourt Brace Jovanovich, p. 40.

8 Helen Keller (1929). *We Bereaved*. New York: Leslie Fulenwilder.

Index

For Product Safety Concerns and Information please contact our EU
representative GPSR@taylorandfrancis.com
Taylor & Francis Verlag GmbH, Kaufingerstraße 24, 80331 München, Germany

9 781041 090304